KATH JEFFERY

Encountering the Light

a journey taken

1951 – 2005

Encountering the Light
a journey taken

a collection of five talks
given to Irish Friends between 2000 and 2004
by

Martin Lynn

with foreword by Rex Ambler

William Sessions Limited
York, England

The publication of these papers has been made possible
through the generosity of the
Robert and Kezia Stanley Chapman Trust.

**These papers have been compiled
in memory of Martin Lynn by Alice Clark
in conjunction with
South Belfast Meeting Ministry and Oversight**

ISBN: 978-1-85072-362-2
Typeset by Compositions by Carn, London

Printed in Bembo Typeface from Author's Disk
by Sessions of York
The Ebor Press
York, England

Table of Contents

Foreword

Rex Ambler

The message of the early Friends was distinctive and clear, and if there was any doubt about it their manner of life made it clearer. But the message was not always welcome. It challenged people to confront themselves and their world more directly and honestly than they had done before. At the same time it offered them the prospect – if they had the courage to open themselves to it – of discovering a truth about themselves that could profoundly change them. Facing the truth would dispel their illusions and open up the true human being that lay hidden beneath them, and enable them to relate truthfully and honestly with the people around them. For those who couldn't accept the challenge it became deeply threatening, and they would then see Friends themselves as a threat. For those who could accept the challenge it was liberating: they became 'the Friends of Truth' who devoted themselves to living by the truth and spreading its message abroad, despite the persecution.

It is a message, however, that modern Friends have largely forgotten. We live in such a different world from that of Cromwell's Commonwealth that we cannot but see the people of that time as strange and alien. Without looking too closely, they seem to us like religious enthusiasts, thumping their Bibles and blissfully ignorant of the great discoveries of science that were yet to come. Modern Friends, by contrast, see themselves as rational, responsible and liberal-minded. They are not likely to be moved by self-revelations supposed to come from a 'light within'. This development over the years is almost inevitable, and much has been gained by it. But have we at the same time lost something?

Martin Lynn's book is written with the conviction that we have. The Society of Friends, he writes, 'is losing its way because it has lost sight of these insights that Fox and his colleagues grasped so long ago when they were defining Quakerism'. He gives two reasons for this. One is the influence of secularisation, which has subtly affected the thinking of Friends, and rendered them speechless in the face of the spiritual reality that is the centre of their lives. The other reason is the pressure towards social and political activity, 'the outer thing', which draws them away from 'the inner thing' of exploring the Spirit. This spiritual life, however, is the very basis of Quakerism, so if that life atrophies Quakerism itself will eventually disappear.

Martin Lynn was an historian, so it was natural for him to ask how this situation came about, and also, more importantly, what it was that inspired and empowered the movement when it first began. So there is much discussion here of George Fox, William Edmundson and other early Friends. But his interest is not purely historical. He is writing these papers – originally given as talks or lectures – in order to bring that early Quaker message to life again. We can quickly sense the intensity and passion of his engagement, his conviction that this seemingly alien way of talking is highly relevant to us, in our very different situation today. When he talks of 'the Light Within' that can reveal us to ourselves and open up new possibilities for our life, we know that he is talking from his own experience, as much as from his study of the ancient texts.

He is unusual as a modern writer in insisting that the way to enlightenment and fulfilment as a human being is tough and difficult. He is not easy with the comfort and ease with which modern Friends seem to approach spirituality. He wants to remind us that the first thing we have to do to make progress in our spiritual life is to face ourselves honestly, recognise our human pride and brokenness, and surrender our egos to the God we will encounter on the journey. This is 'not easy', he tells us again and again. And I think I can discern a shift in his thinking on this over the time that he delivered these talks. Having emphasized 'discipline' and effort early on, he comes later to emphasize 'the inward light' that will enable us to see and inspire us to action. He is also bolder in describing the Quaker experience as 'an encounter with God', yet he also insists that all of us, at some time or other, have a sense of God being there. The Quaker commitment begins when we accept that reality as it impinges on us, and decide to live our lives in response to it. What seems like a heavy emphasis on the courage and strength to face difficulty, turns out to be a very positive message about the possibility of real transformation, both for us and for the world, and about the joy that comes with it.

It leaves us with a question, however, which I suppose we each have to answer for ourselves: how do we access this 'inner light' that supposedly changes us, and how do we recognize it when we see it?

Rex Ambler
Silverdale, Lancashire, 2006

Encountering the Light

Introduction

Kate Philbrick

It is an honour and a privilege to introduce Martin Lynn's writings, which document parts of his journey to becoming a much-respected Friend, who owned the Quaker message deeply within his life. His powerful, pertinent ministry in his lovely, resonant voice was cut short by his tragically early death aged 53 in 2005. Alongside his academic work as a history lecturer, then Professor of African History, at Queen's University, Belfast, Martin leaves this precious legacy of Quaker writing.

Martin Lynn was born in Nigeria, and brought up in the Anglican tradition. His writings throughout reflect the history and theology he studied in London in the 1970s where he met Alice Clark through whom he came to Friends. The way Quakers lead their lives impressed him. Soon after their marriage, the couple moved to Belfast in 1980 and started to attend South Belfast Meeting where they became mainstays of the Meeting. Martin's contribution was lovingly supported and more than complemented by Alice.

My first conversation about religion with Martin took place around the New Year of 1981 on one of his many family holidays in the Lake District. I remember Martin questioned me keenly about my faith, and in particular about the role of Jesus. Martin was seeking his own way. Typically and efficiently he recorded his acceptance into membership of the Religious Society of Friends in his diary on 21 November 1982.

After his convincement, Martin, a generous friend to many, used to send me Quaker books significant to him, notably George Fox's diaries, Rex Ambler's *Truth of the Heart* and Thomas Kelly's *Testament of Devotion*, which he found key to his Quaker development. We exchanged ideas on Quaker practice and ideas as well as talking about our work for Quakers. As an elder in the early 1990s, Martin gave a talk on basic Quakerism. As in his other talks he offers a personal view of Quakerism with his historical analysis. From the maze of very real and difficult questions of defining Quakerism and where to start, Martin, the historian, leads us to Fox: 'If we are looking to Quakerism then we have to look at its founder, at least to start our examination of Quaker beliefs'. This starting point remained with Martin throughout his life: how can modern Quakers reconnect with the living Christ of early Friends?

Martin pursued his interest in George Fox and organised young Quaker study tours to the seat of Quaker history in Cumberland, and accompanied their 'pilgrimage' in 2000. In 2003, although he found it a tremendous strain on his health, he delivered two series of lectures on Fox's work. For Martin, the organised historian, we sense the challenge of ordering Fox's thoughts, which he found 'unsystematic and haphazard'. After a brief chronological background in his talk 'George Fox's Teachings Today', Martin, the considered and considerate university teacher he was, typically digests and extracts five basic texts from Fox's writing.

The Religious Society of Friends in the twenty first century continues to face George Fox's ongoing challenge. However Martin finishes with comfort from Fox himself that with God's help we can allow the truth to set us free. 'You wilt find strength from him (God) and find him to be a present help at time of trouble.' Here as in the following chapter, 'all Friends know the tremendous upsurge of joy they experience', Martin suggests positively and optimistically that others have experienced God at hand as he has. Indeed, that direct religious experience is available to all is a recurrent theme in Martin's work. He returns to this explicitly in 'Seek and Ye Shall Find': 'My belief is that we all in this room – Quaker and non-Quaker alike – have... been aware of the presence of God.'

Not surprisingly given the importance of Meeting in one of the five basic texts extracted from George Fox, Martin wrote a booklet, *Meeting for Worship*, which was printed and made available to Friends throughout Ireland. Characteristically four responses for Quakers are highlighted here: discipline (including preparation), surrender, adoration and joy. He succinctly and humorously describes prayer as 'please, sorry and thank you' thus making complex ideas simple to understand – if not to achieve. Here, when dealing with these more modern concepts, the reader is also referred to other great Quaker writers such as Thomas Kelly and George Gorman. The conclusion focuses on the preparation of hearts and minds for Meeting practically by being punctual, important for Martin who also organised the door-keeping rota, and by seeing Meeting as 'the very core of our week'.

The Ireland Yearly Meeting lecture Martin prepared, 'Seek and Ye Shall Find' [1], develops the final words of the previous chapter from the possibility to 'yearn for and achieve... profound intimacy and communion with God' and looks at 'the need to both seek and find encounters with God'. Martin chose this theme to define the distinctly Quaker encounter with God, and also to focus on Quaker spirituality, the 'inner thing', which he felt could be lost in the deserved Quakers' reputation for good lives and work. Martin himself expressed the 'outer thing' in his life and his service on both

---

[1] Originally prepared for Ireland Yearly Meeting in 2002, not delivered because Yearly Meeting was uniquely cancelled because of the foot and mouth epidemic.

the Africa Committee of Quaker Peace and Service for whom he travelled in Africa, including to Darfur, and on local Quaker committees.

'Seek and Ye Shall Find' questions whether seeking a spiritual experience is enough. The distinctively Lynn message is that early Quakers found God and that 'the inner discernment of God represented by the inner light … is there for all of us if we wish to respond'. He again successfully uses the analytical device of extracting and examining three main aspects of early Quaker 'seeking', and three of 'finding': the inner light, the presence of God now, and the Kingdom of God here. Martin impishly – for he was a funny practical joker – sees himself answering George Fox's question 'what canst thou say?' with 'er, um, well, not very much, George, not very much'. It is a clever way of subtly asking the audience to have more confidence in the Quaker message of 350 years ago, to resist the secularisation of Quakers and to question whether modern Quakers do enough to learn from the spiritual experiences of early Friends, and 'proclaim our own encounters with God today'. Martin is convinced that we can still experience God and our hearts will leap with joy as George Fox's did.

Although reluctant to talk about it, Martin followed the peace process and politics in Ireland keenly. Quakers presented a bold alternative and Martin contributed to Ulster Quakers' peace work through a long commitment to the Ulster Quaker Peace Committee and the Ulster Quaker Service Committee.

Martin's reticence was tested by the British and American invasion of Afghanistan following the New York bombings in September 2001 and he wrote the talk entitled the 'Quaker Peace Testimony'. He was not an overly active protester, but peace was at the core of his beliefs. From his prolific correspondence I feel that military action in Afghanistan and then Iraq eroded Martin's belief in good government in Britain and this disillusionment contributed very significantly to the periodic loss of hope and physical problems Martin experienced over the last few years of his life. Given his clear pacifist principles, the starting point of this paper is in a sense surprising and yet historically correct. Martin scrupulously points to the expedience of Quakers' initial adoption of the peace testimony; he argues that it was only in the nineteenth and early twentieth centuries that Quakers pro-actively owned the testimony offering active support during wars and working to prevent wars. Although Martin's work is peppered with short allusions to his personal life, this paper is the first where he really admits to his personal struggle with being peaceful. For him pacifism is about how we relate to God, the world, ourselves... He ends 'It is very, very difficult.' Martin was a fervent correspondent – requiring answers and developing the concept of the 'netiquette' of emails, which must be answered promptly: my email response to Britain at war had been 'we must do what we do as well and prayerfully as we can'... Martin's was to seek peace within himself and in his actions.

This mature owning of his personal spirituality and life is very evident in the 'Children of Light' which, like his earlier paper, 'Seek and Ye Shall Find' for the cancelled 2002 Yearly Meeting, I had the honour of reading and commenting on before he gave it. Martin did listen to comments, others and mine, and he tested the lecture for coherence with his life. He was very conscious of the honour and responsibility of giving the 350th centenary Ireland Yearly Meeting Public Lecture. As a historian he was well suited to outline Quaker origins in Ireland which he did, stating at the outset that he wanted the 'anniversary to be a time of looking forward with confidence rather than looking back in concern'. During the two years since 'Seek and Ye Shall Find', Martin had suffered a near death illness and therefore had much time away from work for reflection. He could no longer play cricket and climb high mountains as he had, but he had developed spiritually and was 'grateful "beyond what words can utter" that I found Quakerism and Quakerism found me'.

This beautifully structured and polished Public Lecture dwelt on the inner light available to all. 'The Light as encountered by the Children of Light is therefore a spiritual transformation within the individual.' Martin urges the Society of Friends to nurture its spirituality. 'Service, or good works, without the spiritual bedrock of the light become like the house built on sand without foundations, destroyed when the storm comes. For we all can lead accompanied lives and lives of Light, whatever our faith might be and whatever the tradition within which we choose to express it.' I can just see him deciding again that the semi joke about George Fox needs to be repeated: both to get his message across with humour as well as seriously and because for him the real question we all need to answer daily is 'what canst thou say?' Our answer all too often 'er, um, well, not very much, George, not very much' did not satisfy Martin.

'Children of Light' was the name Quakers gave to themselves – but I feel it was also about Martin's own children, Hannah and Megan, whom he had come to love and cherish even more since his illness and for whom he wanted a strong Quaker society in the future. In particular the challenging but optimistic end to his lecture, sadly Martin's last Quaker writing, is for them and for us all, Quakers and others. We must learn from our children and modern Quakers must reconnect with the living Light of early Friends:

'Those Children of Light, like children everywhere, have much to teach us: they question, they challenge, they cause us pain and difficulty as we adjust to their challenges, but they, again like children everywhere, also show trust and faith and love and joy and confidence in the future. Let us… become like children: Children of Light.'

Kate Philbrick is a member of West of Scotland Monthly Meeting and of QPSW Crime and Community Justice Group and Function Group for Children and Young People (Scotland).

George Fox's Teachings Today

This paper was originally given as a series of talks both to Richhill Meeting, Co. Armagh and to Martin Lynn's own Meeting of South Belfast in 2002.

George Fox's Teachings Today

George Fox was a complex man. His ideas may have a very simple message at their heart, but they are not simple ideas. Nor are they easy to unravel. Fox was never a systematic thinker and his ideas were never spelt out in a straightforward way. Rather his writings were produced in reaction to specific situations and he consequently developed his teachings in an unsystematic and haphazard way. This complexity is reinforced by the fact that his ministry lasted over forty years and the emphasis of his teachings, not unnaturally, changed over that period of time. Furthermore, he edited his writings in his old age, cutting out parts he saw as no longer relevant. For us today therefore, unravelling what it was he was saying when he was saying it, is by no means an easy task.

Yet Fox was also a remarkable man with a remarkable, universal, vision. We know he had a powerful, even charismatic, personality that had a striking impact on his contemporaries and indeed on later generations. Some at the time – and subsequently – hero-worshipped him in a somewhat unwholesome way. He was called 'God' by some Friends who prostrated themselves before him; 'thou God of life and power,' said Richard Sale. Others found him – and find him – a dislikeable character: arrogant, pushy, self-righteous and holier-than-thou. Both extremes, however, are unhealthy and both were objected to by Fox at the time. As Rex Ambler has argued in his book *Truth of the Heart,* the paradox of Fox was that he was a teacher who went around teaching that people should not listen to teachers like himself. In truth he was an ordinary human being with all the strengths and weaknesses of ordinary human beings, but with a remarkable insight into other human beings and their spiritual needs, and into the relevance of Christ's message for them.

His was, as mentioned, a long career of ministry. Born in 1624 in the east Midlands, he left home at nineteen and travelled around much of the eastern parts of England. At twenty-three he had his conversion experience, famously described by him as his realisation that there was one, even Christ Jesus, that spoke to his condition. In 1652 at the age of twenty-seven he ministered on Firbank Fell in Westmorland, the moment that is usually taken to be the start of the movement that became known as Quakerism. He married at forty-five, visited Ireland in the same year (1669), travelled to the West Indies and America in 1671-73, journeyed to mainland Europe in 1677 and died in London in 1691 at the age of sixty-six. He published his *Journal,* the main source of his teachings for later generations, in 1676.

My aim in this paper is to outline what I see as George Fox's message to us today, some 350 years after the start of his ministry. I recognise that for such a complex thinker as Fox there will inevitably be different views on the meaning of what he was saying. I do not claim to have the only insight into Fox's teachings nor that my interpretation of his message is an original one. But what I do claim to outline here is *my* vision of Fox and it is one that I find powerful and compelling; it 'speaks to my condition'. I want to outline this vision by first looking at what I see as at the heart of what Fox was teaching during his lifetime and then, in the second part, examining what the implications of this are for us today.

George Fox's teachings

I want to suggest that most of Fox's teachings can be reduced to five key ideas. These were to a greater or lesser extent unique to him and while there is more to Fox than just five ideas these are, in my view, what are at the heart of his message. I want to outline these five ideas in turn, by using five propositions that come from Fox or from the Bible:

i) 'Christ is come to teach his people himself'
(George Fox: Journal p. 155)

In one sense we can now stop our consideration of Fox's teachings. In this one sentence is outlined all that really mattered to Fox or matters about Fox; there is no more important statement in all of Fox's teachings. This idea that 'Christ is come', with its present tense, is *the* central Quaker idea and of more immediate importance to early Friends than the other significant idea of 'that of God in every person' that has come to be the defining characteristic of modern Quakerism. If all of Fox's writings were destroyed but this one proposition survived, then we would still understand what Fox was about. It is a very simple and straightforward idea, yet one that is profoundly revolutionary in its implications.

Fox taught the direct, unmediated experience of Christ. There was no need, he said, for Church, teachers or even ultimately, scriptures: Christ is come to teach his people himself. 'Put not your trust in any child of man, for there is no help in them,' he said. He rejected all outward forms of religion and taught that the inner, personal experience of Christ was supreme.

This was, it should be stressed, a revolutionary idea. Fox's spiritual heritage lay with the Baptists – Elizabeth Hooton and Paul Hobson, both Baptists, were his significant early influences – but his teachings went further than any

Protestant thinker before him in moving away from the authority of Churchly structures and written scripture to the individual experience of Christ. He stressed that sense of direct, personal communion with Christ – of understanding of, and by, Christ – that we all can experience if we wish to. This experience Friends called the Inner Light. We need nothing else, Fox said. 'Your teacher is within you, look not forth,' taught Fox, for 'the Lord God alone will teach his people'. For Fox this idea, of the light of God that illuminated the individual, came from John's Gospel. 'I was commanded to turn people to that inward light, spirit and grace, by which all might know their salvation and their way to God.' Nothing else was needed.

This light was not the same as the individual conscience. Rather, Fox argued that the Inner Light was the spirit of Christ that prompts the conscience. 'You know… when you have wronged anyone,' said Fox, 'and broken promise and told a thing that is not so, there is something riseth in you that is a witness against you – and that is the Light.' We all experience this, he said, we all experience this sense of encounter with God in our lives, the sense that we live an accompanied life, in communion with God – if we want to open ourselves to it.

This Inner Light within us was Christ, nothing more, nothing less, said Fox: as he said in his conversion experience: 'then I heard a voice which said "there is one, even Christ Jesus, that can speak to thy condition"'. Again, in the 'Letter to Barbados' of 1671, he spells it out clearly: 'Jesus is… our foundation… is the propitiation of our sins, and not for our sins only, but also for the sins of the whole world… and… is our alone redeemer and saviour, even the captain of our salvation… neither is there salvation in any other.'

Fox attacked those who only know Christ at second hand. Instead, he made each person's private encounter with God –

the private encounter of each and every one of us – the test of authentic faith. Our own experience is the key. 'None that is upon the earth shall ever come to God but as they come to that of God in them.' Everyone is to come to God 'in their own particulars'.

This was a simple idea and Fox stressed that we should not complicate it. Yet it was earth shattering in its implications: God speaks to everyone who chooses to listen. God will show you *everything*, said Fox: if you choose to listen then the Inner Light will lead you to all Truth.

Moreover this is for all people, he said; all have this Inner Light. It was open to all, even the most hardened criminal, even to each of us reading this. In his famous attack on the 'liars, drunkards, whoremongers and thieves' of Ulverston in 1652, he said that even they had this capacity to know God. Fox never argued for an elite of the elect or saved against the damned; he challenged the Calvinist doctrine of pre-destination and rejected the idea that Christ died only for the elect: Christ died for us all. 'For I saw that Christ had died for *all* men.… I saw that the grace of God which brings salvation, had appeared to *all* men' (my emphasis). This idea, it should be stressed, went beyond the conventional Protestant theology of the seventeenth century that all did have Christ's spirit but did not realise it, and that individuals needed to study scripture to open themselves to it in order to receive the Grace of God and thus salvation; this conventional view relied ultimately on pre-destination and God's choice. Fox turned this round and said this experience of Christ was given by Christ to all; it was our choice as to whether we wish to respond to it. All could experience the Inner Light which was Christ, all could encounter Christ and this experience – direct, unmediated – was all that mattered in our spiritual life.

This teaching of the paramountcy of the Inner Light and of the individual experience of God, raises the issue of scripture and its place in Fox's message. Fox taught that the Word was not more important than the experience of Christ himself. Indeed Fox first came to public attention in England in 1649 when he argued with a priest in a church in Nottingham over the Bible, consequently being arrested for saying that the Jews had scripture but they still crucified Christ; scripture without the experience of Christ he said, meant nothing. In 1674 he famously argued with a group of ministers and lawyers about the Bible and said that the spirit of God was more 'fit and proper' for mankind 'to rule, direct, govern and order their lives by' than the Bible. Many Friends took Fox at his literal word; there are several instances of early Friends burning the Bible at their Meetings in order to convey this point. Famously too, Margaret Fell 'cried bitterly' in Ulverston church when she heard Fox preaching: 'We are all thieves, we are all thieves,' she wept, confessing that she had hitherto relied on the Bible alone, 'we have taken the scriptures in words and know nothing of them in ourselves'. In contrast, Fox's teaching was to rely 'wholly upon the Lord Jesus Christ'. As a child, said Fox, he had a literal knowledge of scripture but 'now I know the scriptures to be true by the manifestations… of God fulfilling them in me'. In short, argued Fox, we must go beyond the Bible to our experience of God.

However Fox never said that we should ignore scripture. As he said, the scriptures 'were very precious to me'. In the 'Letter to Barbados' he makes it clear that the scriptures come from 'the Holy Spirit of God through the holy men of God who spoke… as they were moved by the Holy Ghost'. He refers on another occasion to Friends being, in their experience of Christ, in the same spirit as those who wrote the scriptures. What Fox is teaching is simply that the Word is not more important than the experience of Christ; the Inner

Light must test the scriptures. This was, nonetheless, a challenge to the conventional Protestant theology of the time. His view that scripture and spiritual experience must be taken *together* was a new and provocative one.

The idea that 'Christ is come to teach his people himself' is, therefore, the key original idea of Fox and one that was not extreme or radical Protestantism, but something that went beyond Protestantism to a new view of Christ and Faith. It is a 'Christopresentist' (as the theologians call it) view of Christ that stressed the direct experience of Christ and that was expressed in the early Friends' belief in the presence of God *now* and the Kingdom of God *here*. Hence the revolutionary early Quaker belief that the second coming of Christ was something that happened daily to us all. This controversial idea generated the intense hatred that early Friends experienced. Conventional Protestant theology stressed that Christ was present in his spirit in us all; Fox went beyond this to argue that Christ was present in more than just spirit. 'Doth not Christ dwell in his Saints (i.e. Friends)?' said Fox. It was this that led to the common charge by contemporary critics that early Friends were so-called 'Papists'. It should be noted however, that in time Fox qualified this view. The fate of James Nayler, who did indeed suggest he was Christ, prompted a retreat to a position where Fox argued that Quakers could live in the same power as the Apostles, rather than be the Apostles.

The central idea of Fox therefore – his claim to uniqueness as a spiritual teacher – lay in his teaching of the direct, unmediated experience of Christ: 'Christ is come to teach his people himself.' This is a very profound idea in its implications for how we see Christ and our personal relationship with God. But it begs a fundamental question. How do we react to that direct, unmediated experience of Christ that the Inner Light offers us?

ii) 'And the Lord opened me that I saw through all these troubles and temptations'

(George Fox: Journal p. 14).

I want to try to examine this through the Quaker idea of 'openings'. Early Friends, and not just Fox, repeatedly used the idea of 'openings of the Lord' to explain their encounter with God. Thomas Camm on hearing Fox preach in 1652 wrote that 'my soul was… opened, reached and convinced'. This experience of opening was central to the early Quaker idea of conversion.

What did this Quaker idea of 'opening' mean? The key opening is of course Fox's own experience in 1647, following his struggle with his faith during that period and his 'long dark night of the soul', as we would put it today. These 'troubles and temptations' left Fox in doubt and despair, until he heard the voice saying that Christ Jesus could speak to his condition. In his *Journal* for this period Fox repeatedly uses this term of 'opening' to describe his experiences. He uses the idea to suggest that the Inner Light, i.e. the individual's experience of Christ, will 'open' a person to Christ, if they will let it. However this begs the key question, how do we ensure we experience this 'opening of the Lord'? I want to suggest that Fox urges us not to passively accept the experience of opening but to react in a more positive and proactive way; our discovery that 'Christ is come to teach his people himself' requires changes on our part.

Fox's teaching on how we react to Christ is deceptively simple. 'Wait patiently upon the Lord, whatsoever condition you be in, wait in the Grace and Truth that comes to you by Jesus, for if ye do so, there is a promise to you and the Lord God will fulfill it in you.' However this 'waiting' is not something passive; in actual fact it requires discipline and effort. It requires the discipline of silent worship, which in turn requires spiritual humility and personal change. 'Listen and consider in silence,' says Fox, 'in an attitude of *humility* and you will hear the Lord speak to you in your mind' (my emphasis). This humility requires killing off our own egos. 'Deny thyself,' says Fox, 'and from thy own will… thou must be kept. Then thou wilt feel the power of God… and there the wisdom of God will be received, which is Christ.' Elsewhere he encapsulates it succinctly: 'you must die in the silence…' and again, 'stand all naked, bare and uncovered before the Lord'.

Spiritual humility is therefore the first step that follows once we accept the Inner Light. The stripping away of the ego, of our pretensions and self-image that this requires, is harder to achieve than it might appear. We all love to maintain our own image of ourselves, of what sort of person we think we are. Instead, suggests Fox, this needs to be cast aside. We then need a further and much more difficult step: to examine ourselves with honesty and courage. Rex Ambler terms this a 'struggle of self-judgment' and unquestionably this struggle is right at the very heart of Fox's teachings. Fox stresses our need to accept responsibility for ourselves. We need, he says, to stop blaming others all the time for things that go wrong. As he said on one occasion, in reference to priests and their followers, 'these said it was they, they, they that were the bad people, putting it off from themselves', rather, says Fox, what is necessary is for us to say 'I, I, I, it is I myself', who is at fault. In short, rather than 'putting it off from ourselves' we need to search ourselves inwardly. 'Let the light of Jesus Christ, that shines in every one of your consciences, search you thoroughly and it will let you clearly see': there in a nutshell is the basis of the Quaker 'opening'. 'Be open and honest to the Lord,' he says, 'without any thought of what you yourself may get out of it.' This is needed, if we are, in Fox's words, to pass 'from death to life'. This is inescapable, he says, for 'the great day of the Lord has come… when every heart will be disclosed and the secrets of everyone's heart will be revealed by the light of Jesus'.

To achieve this Quaker 'opening' or spiritual break-through, it is necessary therefore, to admit our failings and to see ourselves as we really are. 'I have examined myself and tested myself and found Christ Jesus in me,' says Fox. This is of course an uncomfortable, difficult and even distressing experience. But then being a Quaker is not supposed to be easy. To pass 'from death to life' is a struggle, a struggle in the harsh search-light glare of the Inner Light, with the Light searching out all the corners of our consciences, revealing all our denials, all our petty selfishness, our ego, our self-deceit and the meannesses that lie within us. Moreover, this is not something that we need to do just once and then it is over and done with, rather this passage 'from death to life' is something we must undertake many times; it is a repeated and indeed constant, process of self-examination and inner struggle.

This raises the issue of 'sin', not a word we modern Quakers feel comfortable with. Yet clearly Fox and early Friends had a concept of sin and it was important in their theology. Fox himself spoke of how he indulged in the 'cup of fornication' before 1647. Again however, Fox breaks away from conventional seventeenth century Protestant ideas of sin in a way that is profoundly impressive. Fox rejected the idea that we were tied by Original Sin to permanent damnation. Rather, central to Fox's ideas was a more positive notion of *overcoming* sin. He had ultimately an optimistic view of humanity that stressed our human potentiality. His view was that having examined ourselves in the glare of the Inner Light and gone through the ensuing struggle of self-judgment, we can experience Christ's spirit and go on to great things. We can, in short, realise our full potential as human beings. If you do commit yourself to this struggle, says Fox, it is a profoundly liberating and empowering experience. You will experience mercy and peace, a new self will be born and you will enter into a new relationship with God.

This new relationship, said Fox, would lead to purity. Human purity was Fox's aim. His aim was to liberate and empower the believer. He stressed that we can become perfect, 'Be ye therefore perfect, even as your Father which is in heaven is perfect' (Matthew 5:48) was a central text for him. He repeatedly stressed this ideal of human perfectibility; a hunger for human perfection was central to his teachings. This optimistic vision of humanity was a vision of what, at our best, we human beings are capable of. His demand for honesty and self-examination is difficult but there is no wallowing in self-reproach in Fox's vision. He believed that we can achieve perfectibility by obedience, by subjecting ourselves to God's power and obeying the light of Christ. He believed human beings could get back to the pre-Fall Adam and Eve, and it was this that he meant when he said he lived in the same power as the Apostles. 'Live in the light which was before darkness was'… and 'in this you will know God's dwelling.'

'And the Lord opened me that I saw through all these troubles and temptations.' The Quaker opening that comes from discovery of the Inner Light is, therefore, not a passive experience that simply happens to us, but rather something that requires intense personal exertion, beginning with spiritual humility and moving through a difficult and painful process of continuing self-examination.

iii) 'Love not the World, neither the things that are in the World'
(I John 2: 15).

For Fox the point was that we have to show how this experience of the Inner Light and the spiritual humility and self-examination that ensues, changes our lives. Fox argued that once you opened yourself to the Inner Light and to the insights and revelations about yourself that resulted, you would be changed fundamentally. If this process of moving 'from death to life' was genuine and you had truly found the Inner Light, then your life would 'speak'; it would change your whole way of life.

At the heart of this for Fox and early Friends was a rejection of 'the World' as it existed in their times. From the start, early Quakerism was characterised by rejection of a profane World. They refused to accept the World's norms: hence their refusal of hat-honour, their use of plain-speaking, their refusal to use pagan names for months and days of the week, their rejection of Christian festivals and so forth. They repeatedly spoke of 'walking' in the Light and this meant just that: a sharp distinction between the Light and the dark and a turning away from the darkness of the World. The Plainness which was so loved by early Friends was valued because it represented a rejection of the World.

Fox and early Friends saw the profane World as something that would contaminate their encounter with God. This attitude reflected the importance they gave to their experience of encounter. Music, dancing and frivolous talk were precisely that: frivolous activities that detracted from humanity's encounter with God. If your life had truly changed you would 'love not the world' and willingly turn your back on these worldly activities.

In place of a life lived according to the World's norms, Fox urged Friends to lead – to walk – a distinctive way of life that showed the World how they had changed. 'And you that do profess the primitive, pure and undefiled religion, which is above all the religions in the World, show it forth in life and practice.' We need, said Fox, to show this in how we deal with others. This is part of our striving for perfection, to become like Saints, 'so that you may all walk as become Saints and Christians, everyone esteeming and preferring one another above yourselves in the truth, in meekness and lowliness of mind and humility, for he that inhabits eternity dwells with a humble heart (Isaiah 57:15)... therefore be careful, fervent, circumspect and faithful in the truth and let your moderation, temperance and sobriety appear to all men showing forth the work of the Lord.' In short, Fox enjoins us to realise that opening to the Inner Light means we must express the work of the Lord in our lives and in our dealings with one another.

Fox uses the term 'live truth' repeatedly. The original name of Quakers was of course, 'Friends of Truth'. The idea of 'Truth' was central to Fox and this was to be expressed in 'living truth'. Truth was not doctrine or words, however, but rather a way of life. 'Everyone is to be in it and to *walk in the truth*' (my emphasis). 'Love the truth more than all.' 'Loathe deceit and all unrighteousness, hard-heartedness, wronging, cozening, cheating or unjust dealing, but live and reign in the righteous life and power of God... doing truth to all... let truth be the head and practise it.' His stress was on living Truth. For Fox, Truth was the reality of God and of God's relationship with us. This is a relationship of honesty and integrity, a relationship of love – of and by God. Quakers must *show* their experience of encounter with God, by living the love of God in their lives.

It was by living Truth – living God's love – and by living plainly (and thus rejecting the World), that you showed that you had changed as a result of your struggles of self-judgment and that your commitment was to higher things: to God's will. It also showed that you experienced the Kingdom of God *here* on earth, *now*, and that there was no distinction between sacred and secular, because there was no secular. By one's changed life, by living Truth, by plainness, one rejected the secular World with all its faults. It is by living God's truth we make life sacred, make our lives sacred and thereby create the Kingdom of God here on earth, in ourselves and through ourselves.

'Love not the World, neither the things that are in the World.' A rejection of the World and what it represented followed necessarily from the discovery of the Inner Light and was therefore central to early Friends' lives. Living up to this is, however, not easy. How do we 'love not the World'? Fox shows us the way:

iv) Friends, keep your Meetings that in Truth ye may reign… and keep in the truth that ye may see and feel the Lord's presence among you'

(George Fox: Epistle 89)

The injunction, 'Friends, keep your Meetings', is a constant refrain in Fox's teachings. There are three reasons for this:

Firstly, Fox saw it as central to the definition of Quakerism. It was his answer to the charge that the stress on the individual experience of God opened the door to Ranterism. The problem of the 'Inner Light' was, of course, the question of how we know that we are responding to the 'right' light? Does Quakerism mean 'anything goes'? This was a common attack on Fox and still is, that by making the individual experience supreme he allowed the individual to do whatever he or she liked.

Fox's reply to this was to say that God never contradicts himself. Thus the Inner Light cannot contradict itself, unlike the religions of the World. This is how you know the difference between the two. Christ keeps our minds on what is eternal and what is eternal cannot be changed. Fox quoted from John 16:13 on this: 'He will guide you into all truth'. But just as importantly, the individual's experience of the

Inner Light had to be tested in a group, to see that it did not contradict itself. This group experience was Meeting for Worship. In this context the individual experience of God and of the Light within, can be confirmed against other experiences of God and the Light within. If what Fox called 'janglings' ensued, then clearly something was not right. But if the contact of different experiences of Christ led to harmony, then Friends would know that this did represent the Inner Light. Only by regular attendance at Meeting for Worship, where different experiences of God could be shared, could this be truly tested.

Secondly, Fox saw Meeting for Worship as good in its own right. Although we can encounter God at all times and in all places, it is in waiting for God in Meeting for Worship – and the silence that represents the stripping away of the World – that we can be most certain of encountering God, of hearing that 'still small voice of calm'. 'When you are met together in the Light,' said Fox, 'listen to it so that you may sense the power of God in every one of you. In doing this you will find your ear being opened to hear the counsel of the Lord God and your eye being opened to see the Lord Jesus Christ among you.' This is an interesting comment of Fox's, that not only mixes up the senses in a very insightful way (*listen* to the Light) but stresses Quaker ideas of 'Christopresentism' (you will 'see the Lord Jesus among you'). It reflects the belief of early Friends that it is in Meeting for Worship that the Kingdom of God appears on earth.

Thirdly, Fox felt that the group was necessary to support the individual in his or her encounter with God. This encounter cannot be undertaken alone. We live, as Quakers, in a community and we depend on the love of each other in our spiritual lives. We are connected by ties of Christian sentiment, and these are reinforced in Meeting. This goes way beyond superficial ideas of 'fellowship', important though fellowship undoubtedly is. In the Light, wrote Fox, 'you will experience a fellowship that lasts forever (I John 1:7) and in this Light you will come to know where God dwells'. Go beyond fellowship, says Fox, to the bonds of spiritual intimacy that he called 'refreshings': that is, the ties of honesty, openness, support, love and intimacy that bind the Christian community. We must use these ties to share our doubts, problems, understandings and joys with each other. 'Refresh one another in the unlimited love of God,' says Fox. Experience the love of God in community and 'know the life of God in one another'.

Thomas Kelly indeed, speaks of these groups of like-minded Quakers able to meet in spiritual intimacy, united by these ties of Christian sentiment and able thereby to love each other spiritually. These groups exist within and between Meetings and indeed know no boundaries except those of the spirit. These groups go beyond time and place and are the way individual Friends come to 'know one another in that which is eternal, which was before the world was'.

'Friends, keep your Meetings that in Truth ye may reign.' It is only by recognising that our faith exists in community that the changes in our lives generated by our individual struggles of self-judgment can best be expressed. By keeping our Meetings we keep our experience of Christ alive.

v) 'Keep the Gospel Order and government of Christ Jesus'
(George Fox: *Journal* p. 631)

For the fifth and final proposition I want to look at Fox's idea of Gospel Order. Fox used the idea of Gospel Order to mean keeping the right structure and business organisation of the various Meetings of Quakers – Preparative, Monthly etc – in short, maintaining the ordered life of a community that revolves around the right organisation of Meetings according to the broader discipline of Quakerism. But the idea also refers to the ordered life of the individual Quaker when that Quaker accepts the Light within. It is this second sense that I want to examine. What I want to suggest is that Gospel Order is the summation of all that has gone before on our journey 'from death to life'.

To understand this, we need to understand that if we live in harmony with the spirit of Christ, we live in harmony with God and with others; both within our Meetings and outside them. This is Gospel Order, the right ordering of our lives, so that we live in harmony with God's will for us. This needs to be expressed in actions, not in talk, in a life of faithfulness to God's Truth and in a life of humility. 'Walk humbly with thy God,' writes Micah (6:8). But for Fox 'there are too many talkers and few walkers in Christ'. Instead of talking, he says, we need to stay in humble dependence on the power and spirit of Christ. If so, everything you do will be done in the spirit of Christ 'so that glory may go to God in the way (we) live (our) lives'.

Living in accord with the spirit of Christ brings us into unity with our God. It also brings us into unity with our fellow Quakers in what Fox called 'the true Church', the community of Quakers, with each spiritually dependent on the other within Meeting and without it. This unity is Gospel Order. In finding love in God's spirit, we find love in each other. If we live in Gospel Order, says Fox, 'no self-will can arise'. Rather, tenderness and gentleness will flow among the Quaker community as each Quaker experiences the love of God in his or her heart. Harmony between Friends and between Friends and God is the result.

This has profound consequences for us all. If we all live in truth – God's Truth, the truth of the Gospel – then, says Fox, the Kingdom of Heaven comes into existence *here* and *now*.

Friends, 'the days of joy are coming,' he tells us. 'The good will overcome the evil, the light darkness and the life death.' And 'we should grasp this hope set before us, for that hope is an anchor for our lives, safe and secure.'

Gospel Order should thus be seen as the culmination of a long and difficult process of change by us as individuals, or, as Fox put it, the journey 'from death to life'. As we can see, all five of these teachings of Fox's are closely linked, with each leading on to the next. The encounter with Christ that occurs when we recognise the Inner Light generates an intense struggle within us as we examine ourselves with honesty and utter candour. In the glare of the Light we cast away our spiritual and personal pretensions. This leads us to express our spiritual experiences in a changed way of life that rejects a profane World. This brings us into a new relationship, not only with God, but with our fellow Quakers; Meeting for Worship lies at the heart of both these new relationships. This is what Fox called Truth, God's Truth. It represents the Truth that Christ taught in the Gospel. Gospel Order is the spiritual and personal harmony that then results between ourselves and God, between ourselves and our fellow Christians and not least, within ourselves that Fox taught occurs when we follow Christ's Truth. Friends, 'Keep the Gospel Order and government of Christ Jesus.'

The relevance of George Fox's teachings today

Are these teachings of Fox still relevant to us today? Ultimately each and every one of us has to answer that question for him or herself. For myself, I think these teachings are still relevant to us all. For me, Fox is still relevant because he takes us back across the centuries direct to Christ and to Christ's teachings. He strips away the accretions of 2,000 years and gets to the 'pure, undefiled religion' of Christ. Fox was a visionary with a remarkable insight into this and, more broadly, into the nature of the relationship between God and the individual, into human nature and into our encounter with God. Fox thus speaks to me because I hear in his teachings Christ's voice across the centuries; this is my experience.

This leaves us with a challenge that reverberates around the world and across 350 years to us today. It is a dual challenge. Firstly, it is a challenge to the Society of Friends which I, like many, fear is losing its way because it has lost sight of these insights that Fox and his colleagues grasped so long ago when they were defining Quakerism. In my view these are not insights specific to the 1650s but eternal, universal insights, as relevant today as at any time in the Society's history. We have drifted a long way from them. I repeat a quotation from Thomas Kelly that I have used elsewhere: 'we are secular and secularism is in our Meeting Houses'. We have a Society of Friends, at least in the North Atlantic world, that is hesitant and unsure of what it believes and that is allowing its doubts and questionings to consume it. Doubts and questions are right and proper and have a place in all faiths, for blind faith is precisely that: blind. My fear, however, is that these things have been allowed to become all consuming – to be welcomed, almost – to the exclusion of all else.

It is a challenge secondly, to us as individuals. Fox sets us all a personal challenge to move along the road 'from death to life' which I have tried to outline here. I don't pretend it is an easy challenge to address but then it was not meant to be easy. The task for us is clear. We have to ask ourselves, how do we measure up? How do *we* fit the five teachings Fox puts before us?

Yet Fox also offers us an answer to our troubles: by urging us to live God's Truth. This is an answer that is profoundly liberating ('the truth will set you free') and an answer that is clear and unequivocal: 'Christ is come to teach his people himself'. Forget everything else, he says, and trust your experience of Christ. It is as simple and yet as difficult as that.

Let me finish by quoting from a letter he wrote in 1658 and which in my view encapsulates Fox's teachings: 'Therefore be still a while from thy own thoughts, searching, seeking, desires and imaginations, and be stayed in the principle of God in thee, to stay thy mind upon God, up to God; and thou wilt find strength from him and find him to be a present help in time of trouble, in need, and to be a God at hand'. 'To be a God at hand'; that has been my experience, and, I venture to suggest, it is the experience of each and every one of you as well.

Meeting for Worship

This talk was first given by Martin Lynn at South Belfast
Meeting in 2000. At the invitation of Lurgan Friends he then
gave it at Lurgan Meeting. Subsequently the talk was
published as a pamphlet available throughout Ireland Yearly
Meeting. In August 2001 it was published in *Quaker Monthly*.

Meeting for Worship

Meeting for Worship lies at the core of our Quaker faith. Silent waiting on God – and the spontaneity of worship that follows – is what makes us distinctive as a church and defines us as a people of God. Throughout the centuries that Quakerism has existed, this silent waiting on God has been our identifying characteristic. At the heart of this is our experience of how such worship leads us into true communion. George Fox captures this when he speaks of 'the baptism that is in Christ with one spirit into one body' (*Journal*, p 134; 1 Cor 12:13). This entering 'into one body' can be seen as a communion simultaneously with each other and with God. It is a gaining of profound intimacy – a mystical extinguishing of our egos as we feel ourselves being gently absorbed into the whole that is the Meeting. As the 'I' of the individual becomes a part of the 'we', we find ourselves reaching a profound intimacy with God. It is the yearning for this intimacy with others and with The Other that is what defines us as human beings.

This intimacy is easier described than reached. How do we achieve this? As Quakers we recognise that we can't just turn up for Meeting on Sunday morning and expect it to happen as if we were turning on the switch for the Meeting House's lights. We recognise that this attempt at drawing close to God requires effort. Not least the deepening of our relationship with God requires, like the deepening of any relationship, the acceptance of rules.

Such rules include the recognition that Meeting is a communal activity and that being late disturbs the worship of others, that in Quaker beliefs, ministry comes not from us but through us and that therefore we must be open to the promptings of the spirit 'from whatever quarter it may arise', including that of ministry that might on first sight seem unhelpful and that the spirit can come to us from the most unexpected directions.

Yet such rules are only the very superficial part of the relationship with God we hope to achieve in Meeting for Worship; they bring us to the door of Meeting, so to speak, but do not take us in to its depths. This requires more effort on our behalf, while realising, like Isaiah, that God will always be there to help us (Isaiah 58:9). Our starting point in this is to recognise that there are no human rules for where we wish to go in worship, that we are going beyond landfall to where there are no human landmarks to guide us.

Further, we recognise that the experience of Friends in Meeting for Worship reveals an immense variety of experiences of God's love for us. Over time we enter Worship in different ways and at different levels of intensity; what might be our experience one Sunday may be very different the next, let alone the next month or year. Equally, Friends often describe their experience of the same Meeting for Worship in very different ways. This is, in truth, Meeting for Worship's great strength – its ability to speak to different conditions of men and women in different ways simultaneously. Indeed we need to draw comfort from this. We are all at different stages of our Journey; sometimes we may find attending Meeting for Worship difficult and our experience of it dry and seemingly empty. Yet we would acknowledge too, that even the dry and apparently empty times can often, in retrospect, turn out to have a purpose and value that at the time was not apparent. We all experience spiritually difficult times when doubts seem near and the temptation to cease attending Worship seems overwhelming. We need to confront those difficulties with honesty and courage and recognise the continuing value, even in such times, of our weekly encounter with the Presence: 'be of good courage and he shall strengthen thine heart' says the Psalmist (Psalm 27).

We would agree that the communion that comes from a Gathered Meeting with us all 'centering down', as early Friends put it, in oneness, reveals that of God in ourselves and in others. George Fox enjoined us to do this: 'Friends meet together and know one another in that which is eternal, which was before the world was' (*Quaker Faith and Practice* 2:35). But how do we achieve this?

It requires four responses on our part. As a starting point we need to recognise that it requires *discipline*, in the sense of discipleship. It requires us recognising that however experienced or knowledgeable we may think we are in Quakerism, we are all novices in our quest to encounter God; we have much to learn and such learning requires intense effort. Thomas Kelly speaks of us engaging in 'quiet, persistent practice' and we need to recognise that Worship requires just that. Regular attendance at Meeting, even in the dry and difficult times, is a starting point of course, but Meeting is more than just a case of turning up at the appointed time and leaving an hour later. We must recognise that in Meeting we are participating, not simply spectating, and that this, far from being a passive activity where we can sit back and let others lead the way, requires effort and engagement on our part. Worship is not something that someone else can do for us; nor is it an activity by individuals separate from the whole.

Worship is a group effort.

Secondly, it requires us to *surrender* ourselves and our own selfish desires to the whole. Only then can we 'know one another in that which is eternal'. This requires us letting Meeting take us where Meeting takes us. This requires us losing ourselves in God's will, through acknowledging that in Meeting we are entering God's presence – and then going wherever He may take us. Again this is not something that makes us passive; on the contrary our Quaker experience is that such surrendering of ourselves to God's will is profoundly liberating and empowering. Fox describes the empowering that this surrender gives us: 'after thou seest thy thoughts and temptations, do not think, but submit: and then the power comes'.

Thirdly, it requires what might best be described as *adoration*. This is the theme of much of Quaker writing, with Friends reflecting how they come to Meeting in awe, fully aware of the experience before them. Like early Friends we can rightly say that we tremble before the Lord. Thomas Green expresses this when he writes that 'the religious life is not a dull, grim drive towards moral virtues, but a response to a vision of greatness' (*Quaker Faith and Practice* 2.07). As we feel ourselves draw nearer to this vision of greatness in Meeting, we recognise our own frailties, our need for God's help and our profound gratitude that such help is always at hand, no matter what we have done or how distant we may have tried to put ourselves from His love. In short, we come to Meeting in awe, an awe that comes from entering God's presence and recognising our overwhelming need for God's love.

But such awe brings with it a fourth response to Meeting, that of *joy*. Thomas Kelly puts this well: 'the response of the soul to light is internal adoration and joy, thanksgiving and worship, self-surrender and listening' (*Quaker Faith and Practice*

2.10). This joy at experiencing God's presence is indeed a long established theme, which we see most aptly in the words of the Psalmist, 'I was glad when they said unto me, let us go into the House of the Lord' (Psalm 122). All Friends know that tremendous upsurge of joy they experience as they approach their Meeting House on a Sunday morning.

Responses of discipline, surrender, adoration and joy are easy to describe, but how do we achieve them in practice? How do we 'centre down' in Meeting? There can, of course, be no easy answer to this question. Just as different people experience Meeting in different ways, so different people use different methods in Meeting to achieve that intimacy with God we all desire. There can be no simple button that we press, nor would we want such. Friends use different and deeply personal ways to enter the communion of Meeting and to allow themselves to be swept away by the currents of Worship. Some Friends use what George Gorman describes as 'Compassionate Thinking' to draw those sick, troubled or unable to be present in Meeting into the Light. Others may meditate on a verse of scripture, others still may bring a problem to place before God. Yet others, simply pray. Prayer is something some Friends find difficult. Perhaps an easier way is to think of prayer not simply as intercession – selfishly asking of God to do what we want God to do to suit our human desires – but rather to think of prayer as Diana Lampen describes it, as listening not demanding (*Quaker Faith and Practice* 2.26). What does God want us to do? What is His will for us? One method is to think of the three spontaneous responses of mortals throughout the ages to the encounter with God: 'Please, Sorry, Thank you'. These words, which some Friends use as their starting point into prayer, articulate the response of many to the sudden and intimate presence of God.

But is even prayer the heart of Meeting for Worship? Is this the way we can be sure of centering down and achieving communion 'with one spirit into one body'? Not alone. By itself, prayer is not enough. There is still more to coming to Meeting and to experiencing God's presence. This is summed up by the words of the old *Advices and Queries* to come 'with Hearts and Minds prepared'. As this implies, it is what we bring to Meeting that determines what we experience in Meeting.

Coming 'with hearts and minds prepared' is difficult and does indeed require Thomas Kelly's 'quiet, persistent practice'. As Friends well know, coming with hearts and minds prepared does not mean coming to Meeting with a pre-arranged piece of ministry. Rather, it means coming to Meeting ready for Meeting, thereby recognising that we are about to experience something, deep, profound and ultimately, life shaking. But how do we do this? On a simple level it can simply mean putting our thoughts in order before setting out to Meeting; some Friends set aside a quiet time without telephone or other interruptions before setting off to Meeting, in order to attune their thoughts for what they are about to experience. On another level, it means ensuring we arrive at Meeting in good time, avoiding arriving rushed or stressed from our journey and unable to enter Worship with the reverence that it requires.

More than that, coming 'with hearts and minds prepared' means a fundamental change in our attitude to Meeting. We often talk of how Meeting prepares us for the week ahead; we speak of how Meeting helps us cope with the stresses and strains of daily life. It certainly does do that, but perhaps it would be better to reverse this relationship, to turn it completely around and see the week as preparation for Meeting, or, as George Gorman puts it, see 'life as preparation for Worship'. This is much harder than it sounds, but infinitely more rewarding. It requires seeing life and Meeting as fundamentally intertwined, certainly, but also, it requires us, consciously and deliberately, to make Meeting for Worship the centre of our week and of our life. In this we need to get rid of the notion that Meeting for Worship is simply something we 'do' on Sunday morning just like we 'do', say, keep-fit on Tuesday or a French class on Wednesday or whatever. Rather we need to rid ourselves of the all too easy attitude to fall into, that sees Meeting as simply another lifestyle choice in a busy life and career. Instead Meeting for Worship needs to become the very centre around which our whole life revolves, the highpoint of our daily life and the very core of our week. Only that way can we ever hope to bring to Meeting that self-surrender and adoration that Fox and early Friends spoke of; only that way can we ever hope to achieve that profound communion and intimacy with God that mystics down the ages, and Friends too, yearn for and so often achieve.

Seek and Ye Shall Find

This was to have been the Public Lecture at Ireland Yearly Meeting in 2001, the year of the Foot and Mouth epidemic. For the first time in living memory Yearly Meeting had to be cancelled. Martin Lynn was invited to give the paper instead in 2002 but due to a family bereavement he was unable to do so. The lecture was subsequently delivered within Ulster Quarterly Meeting in 2002.

Encountering the Light

Seek and Ye Shall Find

This lecture is a study of the Quaker encounter with God. I am aware this is an ambitious task (to say the least), and that I am trying to set down in words something that is ultimately, as early Quakers would have said, 'beyond what words can utter'. Nonetheless I chose this topic for two reasons. Firstly, because like many in the Society of Friends, I feel that we Quakers are too quick to say what we are not, what we don't do, and what we don't believe but we are curiously reticent in defining what we *do* believe. I wanted therefore to take a small step in the direction of defining Quakerism by trying to say what is it that makes the Society of Friends unique as a Church. The best way to do this, I believe, is by trying to define the nature of the Quaker encounter with God since this encounter is, or ought to be, at the heart of what makes us distinctive. Secondly, I picked this subject because I feel Quaker spirituality is sometimes too easily ignored, not least by Quakers themselves. If we are known for anything as a people of God, I suspect it is for our record of 'service' (what Larry Southard once memorably called at Ireland Yearly Meeting 'the outer thing') – in prisons, in peacemaking, in education and such like. The spirituality ('the inner thing') that underpins this and that gives 'the outer thing' its substance, is, I feel, increasingly in danger of being ignored, especially by ourselves. If my lecture has a message therefore, it is to suggest that we Quakers need to remember our mystical and spiritual origins: our encounter, as a Religious

Society, with God.

I have chosen the idea of 'seeking and finding' – the idea expressed in Matthew 7.7 – as my way into this subject. There are four parts to my examination of it:

1) Introduction, which examines what I term 'the Seeking phenomenon',

2) the qualities of 'Seeking' as expressed by the early Quakers of the seventeenth century,

3) the qualities of 'Finding' as expressed by these early Quakers,

4) Conclusions. In doing this I hope to throw light on where our Society is going today; if parts of my lecture provoke or challenge, I hope they do so gently and with the utmost respect for those of different Quaker traditions to my own.

1. Introduction to 'the Seeking phenomenon'

'To be is to seek.' These are the opening words of Douglas Gwyn's recent book *Seekers Found* which, I must quickly point out, I only came across earlier this year when I had already written the first draft of this lecture. It is an excellent book and I have found it invaluable as I have revised my thoughts for tonight. I want to begin by acknowledging the strong influence of Gwyn's insights on my own ideas.

'To be is to seek.' What Gwyn is saying when he uses these words is that 'Seeking' is part of the human condition. We all desire to understand the questions that represent the mystery of life: Why are we here? What is the purpose of life? Why do things happen as they do? How should I live my life in this messy, complex world of pain and evil, of joy and beauty?

This search for meaning is what defines us as human. I believe this spiritual seeking has become more, not less, of a characteristic of humanity, the more science appears to solve the mysteries of the physical world. Similarly, the more human reason appears to provide a solution to the social and material problems of the world, the stronger appears to become the desire for something more to life than the purely material. There is, in my view, a spiritual restlessness within humans that lies in our very essence. New Age Travellers, seekers after enlightenment, the curious, those of all faiths and those of no faith – all share in this restless seeking that characterises the human condition.

Modern Quakers value seeking. It is a 'good' word in our vocabulary. We pride ourselves on being Seekers. Our founders in the 1640s and 1650s were called Seekers before they became Quakers. Many members of the Society of Friends today would prefer to term themselves Seekers, open to the promptings of the Spirit from wherever it might come. We relish the openness, the rationality, the admission of doubt, and the implication of learning, free-thinking, experience and progress, implied in the word 'seeker'.

Yet my theme tonight is that seeking, in itself, is not enough. When seeking becomes an end in itself, it becomes a dead-end, a process going nowhere – which, after all, undermines the whole point of seeking. Seeking, and the openness and learning that come with it, is of course, vitally important for all people of faith if their faith is to remain real and alive and not to become rigid and ossified. Once we cease to be seekers our faith dies. But the idea that it is the seeking itself that matters, that it is better to travel than to arrive, that in a sense there is no destination, that seeking itself is the destination, is, in my view, a very narrow and limiting position to hold. However this is, I fear, an increasing characteristic of modern Quakerism, or at least that variant of Quakerism – and we

must remember that it is by no means a majority in the
broader family of Quakers – to be found in the North
Atlantic world. We modern, North Atlantic Quakers sometimes seem proud to be seekers but not finders, proud to
admit our doubts and questions – and this honesty, it must be
said, is a strength of Quakerism – but reluctant to proclaim
what we have found. This insight was an important sub-theme
of Christine Trevett's 1997 Swarthmore lecture, *Previous
Convictions*. This has had, I believe, insidious effects on the
modern Society of Friends. As Thomas Kelly, the American
Quaker, pointed out more than half a century ago, we have
become a Society of Friends that has allowed its doubts to
essentially secularise us. We are reluctant to use religious
language and curiously reluctant even to use the word 'God'.
This 'post-Christian' Quakerism as it is has come to be called,
is all too happy to describe itself as seeking, but appears to
lack the confidence to assert what it is that it has found. What
I want to do in this lecture is suggest that Quaker spirituality
can find and indeed that it has much to offer. My theme
tonight is best summed up in a well-known passage by
Thomas Kelly: 'For God can be found. There is… a resting
place of absolute peace and joy and power and radiance and
security. There is a divine centre'.

Let me try to show this by turning to Matthew 7.7: 'seek, and
ye shall find', the verse from the end of Jesus's Sermon on the
Mount. This phrase is part of Jesus's triple command to us:
'Ask, and it shall be given to you; seek, and ye shall find;
knock, and it shall be opened unto you'. It is a triple command
– ask, seek, knock – that is short, sharp, striking and urgent
and which reverberates down the centuries to us. It is a
demand that insists on being obeyed ('For God can be
found'). It is a challenge to us all against spiritual
comfortableness, complacency and conventionality. It is a
persistent command – in the present tense – that says we

should not ask, seek, knock once, but continuously. Those who do not seek will not find, it says, those who do not ask will not receive, those who do not knock will not have the door opened to them. It is a call for persistent spiritual seeking and for permanent spiritual awareness, no matter how spiritually dry and dispirited we may sometimes become. Above all, and this is the core of the verse, the call to seek is a call for us to enter a process – a relationship, I would prefer – with God, that once entered will be maintained. It is a call for us to admit our humanity but one that shows us that we can thereby become in some measure divine.

How then, do we go about this seeking that Jesus calls us to in Matthew 7?

2. Seeking

To answer this I want to go back to the original Seekers who founded Quakerism in the seventeenth century. This year, 2002, is the 350th anniversary of that moment in June 1652 which is taken by historians to be the start of the Quaker movement. On 13 June 1652 George Fox began his ministry on Firbank Fell in what is now Cumbria in Northern England. He spoke for three hours that Sunday afternoon out on an open hillside to a crowd of several hundred. Many Quakers of course, would say that Quakerism, in the sense of Quaker insights, long predated George Fox and that afternoon, and that is most certainly true, but that Sunday 13 June 1652 is as good a date as any to mark the beginning of a faith without beginning. It is appropriate therefore for us now, on its 350th anniversary, to examine what it was that happened in that 'Quaker Pentecost' on Firbank Fell, when those who heard Fox preach were energised to spread out across these islands and beyond, to proclaim the message of Quakerism.

As many of you know, those first Quakers on Firbank Fell were part of a vast movement of seekers spread across Northern England in the 1640s and 1650s, a time of revolution, regicide and civil war, a time once famously described by the historian Christopher Hill as 'the world turned upside down'. The most celebrated group of these seekers were those from Preston Patrick, just to the south of Firbank Fell, who were led by Francis Howgill. They had already discovered, before George Fox arrived, the silent worship and the silent waiting on God that later became the most overt characteristic of Quakerism; they had already rejected the conventional stress on outward show and outward forms of religion that defines Quakers. They were also prepared to reject the social conventions of their time whether concerning religion, hierarchy or relationships between genders – early Friends famously saw men and women as equal within and without the Church – and to seek for themselves.

What were the qualities these seekers brought to their seeking on Firbank Fell and thereafter? I want to answer this question by looking at the writings of some of these early Quaker seekers, including George Fox, and to identify the key ideas they expressed in their search for meaning. I appreciate that in a short lecture like this I can only superficially examine ideas that in their fullness were deep and very profound.

i) *human broken-ness*. An awareness of what they termed humanity's 'broken-ness' is the starting point on the spiritual journeys of many of these early Quakers. George Fox's spiritual journey can be taken as typical of many. His journey began, as many here tonight well know, in confusion and spiritual bewilderment. For him, nothing seemed to make sense. His journey seemed a dead-end. 'I was in great sorrows and troubles and walked many nights by myself... great trouble and temptation came many times upon me so that when it was day I wished for night and when it was night I wished for day… and when I was in trouble, one trouble also answered for another… All the world could do me no good.' It is a feeling of spiritual confusion and despair that I think we all have experienced at one time or another, a feeling that there is no hope, no answer, no way out, and that we will never escape from the situation we are in. Yet Fox knew that giving in to this very human despair would be wrong. He knew that the fact that 'all the world could do him no good', that he had doubts, that humanity by itself seemed inadequate to his spiritual needs, that he could not find answers from other people, *did not mean that there were no answers*. On the contrary, his inability to find answers from human agencies was, he recognised, something positive. He had found his journey's starting point.

Isaac Penington, one of these early Quakers, puts this even more perceptively, in my view. He wrote of his spiritual journey in words that echo Fox's, 'I was *broken* and distressed by the Lord… stripped of all in one day. I wandered up and down from mountain to hill, from one sort to another, with a cry in my spirit', going on to recognise the necessity of this experience as part of his journey and urging how best to respond to this spiritual despair 'when the night comes upon thee… be patient and still and thou wilt find breathings after a fresh visitation, and a meek, humble, *broken* spirit before the Lord' (my emphasis). What Penington is saying it appears to me, is that humanity is inadequate ('broken by the Lord') but that this human broken-ness can be overcome if we first accept it and thereby accept our need for help. It is only by recognising this, by recognising our human inadequacy and accepting that we need help from something beyond us, that we will ever begin to heal that which is broken, namely ourselves. It is human pride and our failure to realise our broken-ness that is our problem.

This early Quaker view was not, as is sometimes thought, a

view that began from a concept of Original sin as being the source of human problems. Early Quakers did not greatly emphasise the idea of Original sin, rather they emphasised the need for human purity, in the sense of something impure becoming pure by being taken over by something greater than it. They spoke of 'the Lamb's War' within, which they saw as a war for purity but which we today might see as a war for wholeness, a wholeness that recognises our limitations and inadequacies and our need, if we are to be whole and fully human, for the help of something outside us. Fox, famously, saw this war in terms of two oceans in conflict as when tides off a headland meet: an 'ocean of darkness and death' and 'an infinite ocean of light and love which flowed over the ocean of darkness'. Accepting the existence of both oceans is necessary, for we are human and therefore fallible and in need of help, but we also know which ocean will eventually win.

ii) *spiritual surrender.* The second quality these early Quaker seekers exhibited therefore derives from the first, and I've termed this the idea of spiritual surrender. By accepting our human broken-ness we are taking the first step in surrendering to God's will. We can see this idea at its simplest in those first seekers gathered at Preston Patrick under Francis Howgill, who had already evolved the idea of silent worship and the waiting on God's spirit that Fox took up. It is of course the case that the waiting on God's spirit that characterises the Quaker Meeting for Worship requires at its centre a surrender of the Self, accepting where the Meeting for Worship may take us, as we wait on God's will not on our own. Fox took this seeker idea of waiting on the Lord and stressed precisely that – that it meant surrendering our will to God's – but emphasised that this waiting, this seeking, would be answered. 'Therefore wait patiently upon the Lord, whatsoever condition you be in, wait in the Grace and Truth that comes by Jesus, for if you do so, there is a promise to you and the Lord God will fulfil it in you. Wait upon God in that which is pure. Though you see little and know little and have little and see your emptiness… so wait upon God in that which is pure... stand still in it everyone *to see your saviour'* (my emphasis).

Central to these passages is that the direction of the spiritual journey – where seeking will take us – is not up to us; we need to surrender our will and see where God takes us. We may find things that seem incomprehensible to us but which often, with a later perspective, make perfect sense. The true seeker is one who lets the waves of the 'ocean of light and love' take them where the tide is running. Isaac Penington again: 'Give over thine own willing, give over thine own running, give over thine own desiring to know or to be anything and sink down in the seed which God sows in the heart and let that grow in thee.' This journey of ours is a journey without maps. Surrendering to the ocean implies being carried by the currents and sometimes this may carry us to places where we may seem lost, but it is being lost for a purpose. 'I am lost,' wrote Francis Howgill in one of the most beautiful passages of Quaker mysticism, 'in the incomprehensible being of eternal love.'

iii) *God-hunger*. This leads us into the third element within this early Quaker seeking that I want to emphasise tonight, that spiritual surrender will lead us to a destination. That if we seek God, God will seek us – the message after all, of Matthew 7.7 – is a repeated theme in early Quaker writings. In early Quakers' seeking there was an awareness that humanity's weakness implied the existence of a God beyond human agency: a God 'who is there' as the saying goes. They had what Thomas Kelly famously described as 'God-hunger'. Their seeking was directed to an end, namely to come closer to God: 'This is our religion,' said Isaac Penington, 'to feel that which God begets in our hearts... to be taught by him, to know him, to worship him and to live in him, in the leadings and by the power of his spirit.' Implicit in this was the deep confidence they had that God is with us on our journey, that we do not travel on the ocean of 'light and love' on our own: 'And in the day of his power,' wrote Penington, 'thou wilt find strength to walk with him, yea in the day of thy weakness his grace will be sufficient for thee, he will nurture thee up in his life by his pure spirit, causing thee to grow under his shadow.' The search for God is difficult and demanding, says Penington, yet we have nothing to fear. Know your own weaknesses – your own broken-ness – and be patient and still, wait, and God will find you. If we seek God, God will seek us.

What then, did these seekers find? What was the nature of the encounter with God experienced by those early Friends in that Quaker Pentecost 350 years ago?

3. Finding

In trying to explain what it was that these early Quakers found in their encounter with God, I am very aware that I am now truly moving 'beyond what words can utter'. To define any encounter with God is to try to define the indefinable. To attempt to get round this I want to use early Quakers' own words to show how *they* saw their encounter with what Fox called 'that which is eternal'. I want to suggest that there are some common features in the writings of early Friends concerning their encounter with 'that which was there before the world was' and that these are best understood by the three ideas of the 'Inner Light', the 'presence of God' and the 'Kingdom of God'; I want to examine these three ideas in turn.

i) *The Inner Light*. Perhaps the most central insight of Quakerism, both early and modern, lies in this phrase. It is a phrase we Quakers today often use. But what exactly does it mean? The idea of the inner light was not new to seventeenth century Quakers but it became their chief characteristic and it marked them out from both the Catholic and Protestant traditions of their time. The inner light in the seventeenth century implied a belief in the direct experience of God taking priority over everything else as a source of religious authority, even scripture. Francis Howgill indeed, denied that Matthew, Mark, Luke and John were the Gospel, 'for Christ is the Gospel, yea, the everlasting Gospel', and this idea that the Bible was not the word of God itself but rather the words of the evangelists and that the word of God lay *behind* the Bible, in the inspiration that produced the Bible, can be found very clearly and repeatedly in Fox's writings. For early Friends the key belief was that the everlasting Gospel – Christ himself – could speak directly to the individual in the here and now. This was not through intermediaries – priests or formal ministers – necessarily, nor through the scriptures, necessarily, but rather through the inner light within us all. Here was the central message of that Quaker Pentecost: that God's love, mediated through the experience of the spirit of Christ, lay within the individual, in the individual's capacity to understand the promptings of God within him or herself. 'They said that he (God) was above the skies, calling it heaven,' said William Dewsbury in 1655, 'but I felt the hand of the Lord *within* me' (my emphasis).

In short, the inner light was an inner discernment, intuition or ability – what we today might call an inner potential – to realise in any given situation what God's will might be. It was the inner spiritual capacity we all have to respond to God, if only we would listen to God, and our inner desire to do good to our fellow man and woman. For Fox the inner light was that sense of rightness that we all – even the hardened criminal – have within us. It is most celebrated in Fox's description of there being 'that of God' in every man and woman. This was undoubtedly an optimistic view of humanity, but it reflected both Fox's belief in the 'infinite ocean of light and love' and Francis Howgill's reference to the 'incomprehensible being of eternal love' that I quoted earlier. We can now see why Original sin had only a limited place in this theology.

This inner light is not the same as a moral conscience. It was more complicated than that. For Fox the inner light was rather the awareness of God that illuminated conscience. It represented the direct personal communion with God that all seekers desire. Although we all have this potential, if we ignore God we ignore our potential and we ignore the inner light. 'Dear hearts, harken to it' (the inner light), wrote Fox, '... for if ye love the light, ye love Christ, if ye hate that, ye hate Christ.' For, he went on, in what is *the* single key Quaker insight from this Quaker Pentecost: 'Christ is come to teach his people himself.'

My belief is that we all in this room, Quaker and non-Quaker alike, have, at one time or another – and some of us more often than others – been aware of the presence of God in our lives in the way Fox was when he became aware of the inner light. It is an experience we find difficult to explain, but it is the sense of being 'accompanied' in our lives that we often have – that, as Mother Julian of Norwich, the fourteenth century mystic, put it, 'all will be well, all manner of things will be well', no matter what – that we live not alone, but accompanied lives. For Fox this experience was the inner light, and the sudden awareness by him of this light in his life was the moment he realised that he did not need priests, professors or ministers, nor for that matter scriptures. The inner light had brought him to Jesus directly. Our task therefore, argued Fox, is to cultivate this inner experience and bring it to its fullest realisation. This is best done, he said, by removing the extraneous from our lives and waiting on God for guidance in the silent Meeting for Worship. 'Wait in the Light to receive the power,' he said.

This experience of encounter was open to all and was not restricted to an elite of 'saved' while the rest of humanity were 'damned'. Fox was no Calvinist. The inner discernment of God represented by the inner light was a capacity shared by all human beings and was, he said, the gift of God not humankind. 'None that is ever upon the earth shall ever come to God but as they come to that of God within them – the light that God has enlightened them with.' It is there for us all if we wish to respond.

Isaac Penington was the seventeenth century Quaker who wrote most extensively on the inner light and who, in my view, most completely captures what the inner light means. His spiritual journey was somewhat different to most of the early Friends. Unlike them he came from a wealthy and privileged background and unlike them too, he was relatively old when he came to Quakerism, being in his forties (whatever the situation today in our Meetings, Quakerism in the seventeenth century was a young person's movement). But like them, he found himself spiritually in despair and a seeker: 'smitten, broken, distressed by the Lord' as we have heard. Then he heard Fox preach and it was a turning point in his life. 'This is he, this is he, there is no other. This is he whom I have waited for and sought from my childhood.' What he termed 'the long dark night and thick darkness' was over.

In his writings Penington developed the idea of the inner light in detail. 'There is a witness of and from God in every conscience,' he wrote, 'from this witness proceeds the true and well grounded religion.' The inner light is there in everyone, whatever their religious background. It comes from God not humankind. How do you know this inner light, he asks? You just do. It is something you experience and it is your choice to recognise and accept the experience. In his own case, he showed how he recognised his encounter with God: 'Why thus, the Lord opened my spirit', going on to say that it is by its impact in you that you know when you experience the inner light, 'it is an inward change, by the spirit and power of the living God. It is that which shineth from God in the heart, wherein God is near to men [and presumably women] wherein and whereby men may seek after God and find him.'

What Penington was saying with this concept of the inner light was, it must be remembered, a profound revolution in the religious thought of the seventeenth century. He was postulating that the personal experience of Jesus as revealed in the inner light took precedence over the Church, over priests and formal ministers and ultimately over scripture as well. It is the central, original 'finding' that derived from these seekers in 1652. However it presupposes a second element in the encounter with God experienced by these Friends:

ii) *The presence of God now.* Throughout the writings of early Quakers is their awareness of the presence of God, as mediated through Jesus, in their lives and in the world around them. Having experienced God through the inner light, the awareness of God was a real, tangible and immediate encounter for these people. God's presence was not something they read about in books or listened to in ministry but something they physically experienced. God's presence had the impact of a physical shock on them. It was their desire to tremble at the overwhelming presence of the Lord that led to their nickname, the 'Quakers'. Fox writes of how his moment of surrender to God's will represented 'a great crack' in the earth. Other early Quakers wrote of the 'groans of the spirit', of the gasps, moans and tremblings of religious ecstasy.

This physical and personal earthquake at the manifestation of the presence of God reflected their surrender to God's will, that as seekers they had experienced the Quaker Pentecost. Three hundred years later Thomas Kelly wrote that these early Quakers were 'burning for God', giving up their own wills to do God's will as expressed in the teachings of Christ. This was a physically frightening experience yet also a curiously comforting one: as in Francis Howgill's reassurance that he was lost in 'the incomprehensible being of eternal love'. Becoming aware of the immediate presence of God implied an awareness of God's love for us as individuals, no matter who we are or what we might have done. God's love was both incomprehensible and eternal, but was there for us all. He was a God who was there. This was the central mystery of the Christian faith and the central message of these early Friends.

Early Quakers explained this mystery in terms of the Second Coming of Christ: 'for Christ is come to teach his people himself'. We could all have a direct personal relationship with Christ. Moreover, this Second Coming was not something that would happen in the future, but was something that was happening now, immediately, that happened and happens as soon as we open ourselves to the presence of God. Fox wrote of a 'new Creation' that would replace the old Creation and that would thereby close the gap between God and humankind (the broken-ness of humanity that derives from our human inadequacy). This new Creation occurs precisely when we realise that 'Christ is come to teach his people himself'. This new Creation ends the alienation of humankind from the presence of God, that alienation from God that derived from the very fact of our *human* nature. This experience of a new Creation – of a new humanity – is something we can all experience and experience now, in the immediate present and not the future. It is a new Creation that occurs within our hearts when we resolve to slough off the old self with its egotism and selfishness and open ourselves to Christ. This new Creation, is the transformation of our selves that occurs at that moment we become aware of the presence of God in our lives. It is an inner apocalypse, or what Douglas Gwyn calls 'the Quaker apocalypse'.

'For Christ is come to teach his people himself', with its *present* tense, is thus the single key Quaker teaching. The realisation of the meaning of those words – that the Second Coming of Christ occurs now in the present and not the future – was the pivotal moment in the emergence of Quakerism, the real Quaker Pentecost on Firbank Fell. It is also the pivotal moment in all our lives. It is that moment when the inner light makes us aware that we live, all of us, accompanied lives and that we are not alone on this earth. It is the moment we realise that God *is*, and that life has a purpose, even if that purpose seems at times incomprehensible. The fact that we are aware that we lead accompanied lives, that we travel 'lost' in Francis Howgill's 'incomprehensible being of eternal love' is our purpose.

The immediate presence of God – as mediated through the inner light – is thus the second element of the insights of early Friends that I wish to emphasise in this lecture. In essence it is the insight that the encounter with God is timeless and beyond time. For these early Quakers, in their new relationship with God, *time* and its manifestations (past, present and future) were fused as one in the *now*. Thus the third element of their teaching I want to highlight tonight is that the encounter with God lies beyond *space*. I've called this:

iii) *The Kingdom of God here*. For early Quakers the Kingdom of God was something that was to be experienced here on Earth and not in heaven ('above the skies' as William Dewsbury put it). The Second Coming was something that happened in the present time, but it also happened in the world, creating, as Fox said, a new Creation here on earth. Francis Howgill again: 'All was overturned... and then I saw the cross of Christ and stood in it... *and the new man was made* and so peace came to be made' (my emphasis). He is saying here that humans can change here and now, can transcend their humanity, and that this is not something that has to wait for a resurrection in the future or in heaven. He continues: 'and the Lord appeared daily to us, to our Astonishment, Amazement and Great Admiration, in so much that we often said one to another with great joy of heart "what, is the Kingdom of God come to be with men?"'

These Quakers identified this Kingdom of God as existing here in a corporal reality on earth and they found it in two experiences. One was in the inner light already mentioned. This was explained, as we have seen, as the presence of God within people; 'that of God within' as Quakers say. This reality represented a personal communion of deep intimacy between the individual and God, that could be experienced by anyone at any time and in any place. This was the sign of Christ's return to earth – the Second Coming – as a present reality. The Kingdom of God existed within each and everyone of us, said early Quakers, and could be identified in our individual capacity to find God and experience his living reality in our lives. The second experience lies in community. For early Quakers the Kingdom of God was to be experienced in the solidarity of the Christian community, among Friends, in Meeting for Worship and outside it. As Howgill's statement about the Lord appearing 'among men' reveals, a solidarity emerged in the ties of Christian sentiment between like-minded people seeking God together, so that God's presence became real and the Kingdom of God thus existed in tangible, incarnate form ('What? Come to be with men?'). In this dual experience, personal and communal, God's presence becomes a reality and we experience a living Pentecost, not once in Palestine or once on Firbank Fell but repeatedly, everyday and everywhere. God's presence can be found wherever we choose to look.

In these two ways – the individual's experience of the inner light and the individual's experience of communal worship – we overcome the alienation of the individual from God and the human broken-ness those seekers identified. Fox's new Creation comes into being with God's presence a reality on earth. We 'atone' for the alienation between God and humanity that Jewish writers ascribed to the expulsion from the Garden of Eden. We experience a transcendent God that exists in the world, just as the first disciples in Galilee did. In this we achieve an intimate unity between humanity and God, a unity that lives the Kingdom of God here on earth in God's time and in God's space.

It was thus a triple experience that these Quaker seekers experienced 350 years ago in that Quaker Pentecost on Firbank Fell. The inner light, the presence of God now and the Kingdom of God here, are the three elements that represent their finding of God. This experience it must be admitted does not come easy to the seeker. It requires an acceptance of our broken-ness and our human limitations if we are to know God. In short, it requires us to accept our humanness – our humanity – but in doing so, the Quaker encounter suggests, this bring us the presence of God. To *seek* is to be human, but to *find* is to go beyond our human nature to something beyond humanity, to an encounter with God that transforms us all. For the reconciliation that early Quakers achieved, I believe, was not simply between humanity and God but also within humanity, between individuals and, just as importantly, within ourselves. This reconciliation was not something that occurred 'above the skies' or in a future resurrection but here and now. It is an inner apocalypse indeed, an inner transformation that early Quakers strived for, one that changes how we relate to God and changes us as people. Like Howgill we can exclaim, 'what, is the Kingdom of God come to be with men?' 'It is, Friend,' we reply, 'for Christ is come to teach his people himself.'

4. Conclusion

In conclusion I would ask what does this examination of the spiritual journey of early Quakers from seekers to finders – of their encounter with God – tell us today? I think it tells us three things.

i) The promise of Matthew 7.7 ('ask, seek, knock') can be and is fulfilled. Seeking does lead to finding; the experience of early Quakers shows us that. As Thomas Kelly said, 'For God can be found.' Jesus's promise is precisely that, a promise that God can be found if only we choose to look. 'Ask, and it shall be given to you; seek, and ye shall find; knock, and it shall be opened unto you.' That message still reverberates down the centuries to us.

ii) I believe that the experience of early Quakers tells us that we have a desperate need to cultivate our spirituality, that which Larry Southard termed the 'inner thing'. Not at the expense of the 'outer thing' (service to our fellow human beings), but alongside it. As Christians, we ignore our spirituality at our peril. Service, or good works, without the spiritual bedrock of 'the inner thing' become like the house built on sand without foundations, destroyed when the storm comes. The Quaker transformation from seekers to finders in 1652 shows us that life in this world is about an encounter with God, an encounter in the here and now, in the present time and in this place. It shows us that the Second Coming has arrived, that it occurs every minute of every day. God is immanent in the world, not just 2,000 years ago in Galilee but today in Lisburn as much as anywhere else. The spiritual world and the material world are one and the same. For we all can lead accompanied lives and lives of faith, whatever our faith might be and whatever the tradition within which we choose to express it.

iii) I speak finally to the Quakers in this room. I speak as a Quaker and as someone who is grateful beyond words that I found Quakerism and Quakerism found me. This study of our Quaker forebears, I hope, tells us that we have a precious heritage that we would be foolish to ignore. This year we celebrate – in a modest and Quakerly fashion – the 350th anniversary of that Quaker Pentecost of 1652. We must, I accept, go forward as a Society and not spend our time looking backwards. But 350 years is an appropriate time to reflect on where our corporate faith is heading. Those early Quakers still speak to us down the centuries. Are we listening? We are members of a Society of Friends that has become, in my view, essentially secularised, that has become, as Thomas Kelly put it more than half a century ago, 'mildly and conventionally religious'. We have become, in the words of Harvey Gillman (a contemporary Quaker), 'a well-intentioned social club of like-minded, nice people'. That is not meant as a compliment. Thomas Kelly again, 'We are secular and secularism is in our Meeting Houses.' Christine Trevett is right, that if George Fox was to reappear among us and ask his celebrated question, 'what canst *thou* say?' our answer all too often would be 'er, um, well, not very much, George, not very much'.

We Quakers have a precious heritage of revelations of an encounter with God, of a seeking that led to a finding on Firbank Fell in June 1652. We need to have more confidence in proclaiming the lessons of that encounter of 350 years ago and of our own encounters with God today. For I am convinced that Christ is indeed come to teach his people himself. If we do so proclaim, if we recognise that the encounter with God can be experienced ('found') by us all, then I am also convinced that, like Fox in one of his most celebrated phrases, our hearts 'will leap with joy'.

The Quaker Peace Testimony

This talk was written by Martin Lynn in late 2001 and delivered to South Belfast Meeting early in 2002 when the world was in the shadow of the events of 11 September 2001.

The Quaker Peace Testimony

'We utterly deny all outward wars and strife, for any end, or under any pretence whatever; this is our testimony to the whole world. The Spirit of Christ by which we are guided is not changeable, so as once to command us from a thing as evil, and again to move unto it; and we certainly know, and testify to the world, that the Spirit of Christ, which leads us into all truth, will never move us to fight and war against any man with outward weapons, neither for the kingdom of Christ, nor for the kingdoms of the world.'

Declaration from the harmless and innocent people
of God, called Quakers, 1661

The Peace Testimony is central to Quakerism. We are one of the four historic Peace Churches and although Quakerism is now becoming increasingly fractured into different varieties around the world, the Peace Testimony is the one thing – perhaps the only thing – all the several traditions of Quakerism still agree on. The Peace Testimony may be said to define us as a Church.

My purpose in this piece is to examine the importance of the Peace Testimony for the Society of Friends. I am going to argue that it rightly has a significant place in our traditions, but, I will suggest, we give it too much importance. We put it into a Glass Case and revere it, while ignoring what the Peace Testimony means, in practice, for us as individual Quakers. I want to show this by examining the Peace Testimony in two ways, firstly by looking at the Corporate Witness of the Society of Friends – how the Society of Friends as a whole has interpreted the Peace Testimony – and secondly by looking at the implications of the testimony for us as individual Friends, in what can be called our Individual Witness.

The Corporate Witness of the Society of Friends

Our starting point has to be January 1661, when George Fox and eleven other prominent Friends issued the Peace Testimony (*above*) to King Charles II. This declaration was in response to accusations that Friends were involved in a plot to overthrow the King. In rejecting these accusations, the declaration worked and Friends have ever since been recognised as pacifists. Yet the declaration has led to a myth, that Friends' pacifism was there from the start. In fact this was not the case. Friends served in Cromwell's army in England and in Ireland and occupied very senior positions as officers within it. Fox, referring to these troops, boasted that one Quaker soldier was worth seven ordinary soldiers, a statement we Quakers tend to ignore. Indeed even after the declaration of the Peace Testimony, some Quakers were prepared to use violence for political ends, as in the notorious Kaber Rigg plot of 1663. In short, for the earliest Friends, pacifism was not an absolute and 'the outward weapon' had its place in forwarding God's purpose.

It was simple expedience – the need for survival – that lay

behind the 1661 declaration; pacifism was a necessity if the Society of Friends was to avoid being crushed by the King in the difficult years after the restoration of the Monarchy. This simple historical fact, it can be suggested, is the reason why the Society of Friends gave the Peace Testimony such prominence in its early years, and why, as a consequence, we as a Society have put the Testimony on such a pedestal ever since. In turn the result of this, I would argue, has allowed us often to ignore the implications of the Testimony for ourselves as individual Friends.

It was also these circumstances that meant that the initial interpretation of the Peace Testimony by the Society of Friends was essentially a *negative* one. The Society was simply against war and violence. Friends refused to participate in wars and renounced any involvement in the preparation for war. Hence over the years individual Friends have gone to jail or faced execution rather than serve in military forces; the creation of the category of Conscientious Objector in World War I was specifically in order to accommodate Friends' strongly held beliefs in this matter. More recently, in the 1990s in Britain, a number of Friends have chosen to go to jail rather than pay that portion of their taxes that are used for military purposes, seeing the paying of taxes for military ends as inconsistent with our Peace Testimony.

It was only in the nineteenth century that Friends realised that this negative Peace Testimony simply but firmly rejecting war and violence needed to become a *positive* one, that renouncing violence was not enough. This change to a more pro-active Testimony occurred in two ways. Firstly, Friends realised the need to become involved in the relief of the suffering caused by war. During the Crimean War between Britain and Russia in the 1850s, for example, Friends were involved in relief work in Finland. Perhaps the key moment was the Franco-Prussian War of 1870-71 when London Yearly

Meeting established the Friends War Victims Relief
Committee to deal with the suffering in France; it was at this
moment that the famous Black and Red Star symbol became
associated with Friends' relief work. During World War I the
Friends Ambulance Unit (FAU) was established and some
1,000 individual Friends served in it as medical orderlies and
stretcher-bearers, working in the dangerous conditions of the
front line and in no-man's-land; twenty-one Friends in the
FAU died during the war. Immediately after the war, Friends
were prominent in work among the refugees of central
Europe; one example was Hilda Clark in Vienna. During the
1930s Friends undertook relief work in the Spanish Civil War
and in China. When World War II broke out, the FAU was
reborn and Friends served across the globe, in Egypt,
Ethiopia, Burma, China, India, Germany and elsewhere, again
in the most difficult and dangerous conditions; Gray Peile of
Richhill Meeting worked with the FAU in China in this
period. In 1947 the Nobel Peace Prize was awarded jointly to
Friends Service Council of Britain and American Friends
Service Committee in honour of their work during the war.

The second change in the understanding of the Peace
Testimony during the nineteenth century came with the
realisation that Friends needed to become involved in
preventing war. This required Friends' involvement in
mediation and reconciliation work. This was seen, famously, in
the Crimean War when Joseph Sturge visited St Petersburg in
order to try to mediate between Britain and Russia.
Thereafter Friends were prominent in supporting the League
of Nations and the United Nations and can nowadays be seen
in the Quaker UN offices in New York and Geneva. Other
Friends realised the need to be involved in work to relieve
the poverty and injustice that is often the cause of war.
Friends Service Committee (FSC), and later Quaker Peace &
Service (QPS), were deeply involved in this. Individual

Friends were involved in the setting up of Oxfam, the Fellowship of Reconciliation, the Campaign Against the Arms Trade and many other organisations. Others worked tirelessly for these and other organisations around the globe. Nearer home, we can think of the work of Will Warren in Derry/ Londonderry at the start of the troubles, of John and Diana Lampen and of Steve and Sue Williams.

Our Corporate Witness as a Society of Friends against war and violence is a heroic one, and one of which we can justly feel proud. The awarding of the Nobel Prize is indeed a remarkable achievement. However we can sometimes, as a Society, overplay this story. We feel proud of and comfortable with our Corporate witness but ignore the implications of it for ourselves in our daily lives. There is danger of us falling into 'telescopic philanthropy', where we get terribly concerned about what the Society is doing 'over there' but ignore what we ourselves are doing much closer to home in our own lives. London Yearly Meeting in 1804-05 realised the dangers of such a contradiction when it wrote: 'Now Friends... how do we long that your whole conversation be as becometh the Gospel; and that while any of us are professing to scruple war, they may not in some parts of their conduct be inconsistent with that profession!... be peaceable your-selves, in words and actions'. We need next therefore, to examine the implications of the Peace Testimony for ourselves as individual Friends.

Our Individual Witness as Friends

There are two issues that need to be examined in relation to Friends' individual witness as pacifists. One is the spiritual justification of pacifism and the other is what this implies for us as Quakers.

i) Firstly, what is the spiritual justification for pacifism?

Many reasons can be put forward to justify pacifism. A Humanist would justify it in terms of its benefits. Society would not work unless there is respect for nonviolence. The alternative is the law of the jungle. This is a simple utilitarian argument. Violence does not work. Moreover, the Humanist would argue that as human beings we all share a common humanity and that therefore we owe the same treatment to others as we do to ourselves, precisely because, as humans, we are all the same.

The Christian would agree with this but go beyond it to base his or her pacifism on the fact that Christ's teaching is 'uncompromisingly pacifist' (Reinhold Niebuhr). The Sermon on the Mount in Matthew and the Sermon on the Plain in Luke are unequivocal. The teaching of the Beatitudes ('Blessed are the peacemakers') reinforces this as do other parts of Christ's teachings: 'Love your enemies; turn the other cheek; go the extra mile; give your cloak as well; love God and love your neighbour as yourself.' Paul in Romans, chapter 12, urges us to 'resist evil with good'. These principles are unqualified. Compassion, forgiveness and healing: these are the watchwords of Christ's teachings. Further, it is not just his teachings but his life that is important in this. In his death he reinforced this message, spurning the disciple's sword and accepting death rather than use violence. He willingly chose the Way of the Cross.

Quakers would agree that an uncompromising pacifism was central to Christ's message, but would take the argument a step further. This is the Quaker insight of there being 'that of God' in every person. Quakers would hold that there is something precious and God-like in every person, that their very humanness is God-like; we all have a capacity to achieve communion with God and respond to God's love, we can all become 'Christ-like'. This is what, to a Quaker, makes all human life sacred. To use violence therefore is to negate the very sacredness of life, both in our opponent and in ourselves.

Thus the Quaker view is that Christ's injunction to love our neighbour is an Absolute, and that we cannot pick and choose from his teachings. This acceptance of the absolute nature of Christ's injunctions does, of course, cause problems. Sometimes we face such utter evil, as in the events of 11 September 2001 or in the Holocaust, that we wonder whether in this particular case violence is a necessity, to prevent a greater evil taking place; there are those Friends who have argued that sometimes, sadly, this is indeed the case.

These are serious difficulties that all Friends have to wrestle with. I find difficulty dealing with these ideas myself. But Christ never promised that things would be easy or simple. We too in our lives have to walk the Way of the Cross as he did, with all that that implies. The promise is not that this is an easy way but that it is the correct one: that violence simply breeds more violence, creates more problems than it solves. If we allow ourselves to pick and choose our pacifism from Christ's teachings then the question arises, who picks? who chooses? If we allow that, then that leads us to the idea that 'might is right' – as we have seen in Afghanistan in recent weeks. For a Quaker, pacifism is not a choice.

ii) Secondly, what does this mean to us as individual Quakers living real lives in this messy, difficult, complex world, full of messy, difficult and complex relationships?

It requires two things.

Firstly, it requires an understanding of just what Peace means. It is an old Quaker insight that Peace is not just an absence of violence. It requires an absence of violence, certainly, but Peace is much more than that; the absence of violence is a starting point, but no more than a starting point on the road to Peace. We need to go beyond the absence of violence if we are to discover what Peace really is.

The Quaker belief is that Peace means the expression of God's love here on earth. Indeed Early Friends said that Peace would result from the creation of the Kingdom of God on earth. That is, not in the future but Here and Now, in this world, at this time and in this place. The Early Quaker belief was that the Kingdom of God was not 'up in heaven' to be reached sometime in the future but was present in the here and now: tangible, accessible, palpable, here.

It is accepted that this is not necessarily achievable in full. The Quaker belief is that Peace is a process: a way of going about things. As Sydney Bailey said: 'Peace begins within ourselves. It is to be implemented within the family, in our Meetings, in our work and leisure, in our own localities, and internationally. The task will never be done. Peace is a process to engage in, not a goal to be reached.' To put that another way, Peace is how we relate to the world and how we relate to each other. It is particularly about how we relate to each other.

Secondly therefore, it requires an understanding that the Peace Testimony is about relationships: about *us* in the Here and Now. Peace is not the responsibility of others to establish somewhere else or sometime in the future. It is not simply about resolving a civil war in Africa, say, though it certainly involves that too. I return to Sydney Bailey: 'Peace begins within ourselves'. It means we must recognise our role in the world, our use and abuse of power in relationships and the way we exploit others at home and abroad, within the family and outside it. This requires us to live Peace in our daily lives. We must express the peacefulness that lies in our relationship with God in our relationships with each other, and that means in all our relationships. I recall Ross Chapman of

Bessbrook Meeting once, very rightly, saying that the Peace Testimony was about how you drive your car. It is indeed about how you drive your car and about how you do everything else in your life.

This living of Peace requires reconciliation: with ourselves, with others and with God. We can only achieve this by recognising our human weakness and therefore our need for God's help – precisely because we are human, for as humans we are weak and fallible. We need to recognise this and thereby recognise our full humanness, with all its strengths and weaknesses. And this requires us asking for forgiveness, from ourselves, from each other and from God.

This is not easy. Words like reconciliation are easy to use but very difficult to live up to. The pacifist is indeed called, like Christ himself, to carry a Cross. We can only carry that Cross by recognising our need for help: from God and from each other, in Meeting and outside it. Only then can we achieve the Peace that is the Kingdom of God on earth. Only then, as it says in Numbers, chapter 6, will 'the Lord lift up his countenance upon thee and give thee peace'. But thereby we transcend violence, just like Christ did, and achieve peace. This is, in my view, very, very difficult indeed to achieve but, I would argue, all the more rewarding because of it.

[All quotations from *Quaker Faith and Practice* (chapter 24) unless otherwise indicated.]

Children of Light

In 2004 Martin Lynn finally delivered the Public Lecture to Ireland Yearly Meeting in Newtown School, Waterford. This was the year Irish Friends celebrated 350 years of Quakerism in Ireland.

Children of Light

In the early 1650s William Edmondson, from Westmorland in North-West England, a 'man valiant for truth on earth' and a soldier in the parliamentary army, arrived in Ireland. He was invited over by his brother, a soldier in the English army in Ireland, to set up as a shopkeeper. Edmondson's original plan was to settle in Waterford but he stopped initially in Antrim and having sold the goods he had brought with him returned to England for more. On this visit to England he met James Nayler, one of the leaders of the burgeoning Quaker movement and was (as Quakers say) 'convinced'. On his return to Ireland, he moved in early 1654 to Lurgan where he set up a new shop. As he wrote in his journal, 'my brother being convinced of the Truth... my wife, he and I met together twice a week at my house; in a while after four more were convinced and then we were seven that met together to wait upon God and to worship him in spirit and truth'. So the first Quaker Meeting in Ireland was born.

Later that same year near the village of Kilmore, in Co. Armagh, Margery Atkinson, a widow, 'a tender, honest woman' who 'lived and died in the Lord', began a Meeting for Worship in her house. And so the second Quaker Meeting in Ireland – Ballyhagan (now Richhill) Meeting – was born. The Quakers in this room tonight are the direct descendants of these two Meetings established in 1654.

We know little of Margery Atkinson, but a good deal about William Edmondson. From Lurgan he moved to become a farmer in Co. Cavan and eventually settled near Mountmellick in Co. Laois. Throughout his time in Ireland he travelled repeatedly and extensively (as Quakers say) 'in the ministry', particularly across the province of Ulster, in the Midlands and to Dublin. 'Many people were convinced and Meetings increased mightily,' he wrote. One estimate speaks of 100 Meetings by the start of the next century. He accompanied George Fox when he visited Ireland in 1669. He was arrested numerous times, put in the public stocks in Belturbet and was abused and physically attacked repeatedly. In the 1670s and 1680s he travelled on several visits to the West Indies and North America; he held the first Meeting for Worship in Pennsylvania and in New York City. He is rightly described as 'the apostle of Quakerism' in the Americas; arguably he is of as great a significance in American Quakerism as he is in Irish. He also travelled widely in the ministry in England. He died in 1712 aged eighty-five and was buried in Co. Laois.

Other Friends played important roles in the establishment of Quakerism in Ireland – Francis Howgill, Edward Burrough, Elizabeth Fletcher, Elizabeth Smith and Richard Clayton to name but a few – but it is with these two Friends, William Edmondson and Margery Atkinson, that we see the start of that movement that has brought us together here tonight. It is their legacy, and how we Quakers have discharged it, that I want to address in this lecture.

I don't for one moment pretend that the legacy of Quakers in Ireland is entirely benign or even neutral. After all, the earliest adherents to Quakerism in Ireland were, put simply, soldiers in Cromwell's army, with all the baggage that that brings for Irish people. They were part of that huge expropriation of Irish land that was reinforced by Cromwell's settlement in

Ireland. If we Quakers here tonight are the descendants of these first Friends then we have to accept that part of our history. But if we acknowledge that, then we can also say that Friends have contributed much to Irish society since the 1650s. Their relief work during the famine of the 1840s is widely acknowledged, but there is plenty more that is deserving of commendation. Quakers have been prominent in education with the Friends' schools in Ballitore, Mountmellick, Lisburn, Newtown and elsewhere, in social work, such as among Travellers, in the work of the Ulster Quaker Service Committee, in peacemaking during the Troubles, in work in hospitals for the elderly and infirm. Quaker work in Irish industry is also remarkable: pioneering Irish steam-shipping in the 1820s, and being behind the first steamer to cross the Atlantic in 1838; inaugurating railways in Ireland in the 1830s, in building Portlaw and Bessbrook villages, in iron works in Waterford, in pioneering work in manufacturing like biscuits, in retailing such as coffee and so forth; the list is a long one and I don't pretend it is complete. In case after case, whether in social work or in business, Quakers pioneered the way that others later followed. I think it is fair to say that Irish Quakers have contributed much to Ireland over the years and that these immigrant descendants of Cromwell's army have come to terms with Ireland and, by and large, come to terms with their Irish identity. Indeed given the numbers involved – probably little more than 5,000 at their peak in 1720 – and given that much of their work was driven by a handful of Quaker families, whose literal descendants sit in this room tonight, this is a remarkable story.

It is, of course, also a familiar story and well known to many in this room. But it is a story that, as I outlined it above, lacks a vital ingredient. What drove these Friends? Why did they do this? What was the Quakerism that they professed? What I want to do tonight is to try to answer these questions by looking at the beliefs of these Quakers in the 1650s when Quakerism emerged. I want, in a sense, to try to define Quakerism, something that Quakers are always reluctant to do (and perhaps with good reason). Although my method will be historical – examining the beliefs of the founders of Quakerism – this exercise is not intended to be simply of historical interest. I do it in order to reflect on Quakerism's condition in its 350th year. Quakers, traditionally, take little notice of the world's dates and anniversaries, even one as significant as a 350th. Yet I feel anniversaries have the benefit of prompting us to reflect and this is no bad thing. It is as part of this process of reflection that this lecture is designed as a contribution. This is, I realise, supposed to be a Public Lecture and I apologise to the non-Quakers here for the prolonged bout of Quaker navel-gazing that follows.

So my aim in this lecture tonight, in paying tribute to William Edmondson and Margery Atkinson, Quakerism's founders on this island, is to define what I see as the essence of Quakerism, by examining what moved these Early Quakers on a spiritual level. I should state here that, given the relatively limited writings by Irish Friends in the first decades of Quakerism that I have been able to find – and this reflects my ignorance not theirs – I am using the works of the founding Friends more broadly in these islands: George Fox, Isaac Penington, Francis Howgill and others, to reflect the ideas that Edmondson and Atkinson shared. I should also say at the outset, that I will not speak about the service traditions of Quakerism, not because I don't see these as important, but because I feel this service tradition derives ultimately from the ideas about humanity and its relationship with God that these Early Friends expressed. I want to challenge and provoke, though I do so with no desire to offend. I ask the question: will there be a 500th anniversary of Quakerism in Ireland, or even a 400th? But I also want to try to suggest a vision for the future and to be positive; to suggest that our Friends William Edmondson and Margery Atkinson have much still to say to us in the year 2004 and that this anniversary should be a time of looking forward with confidence rather than looking back in concern.

I want to use the term 'Children of Light' as my way into this definition of the essence of Quakerism. The term comes from John 12.36 (and also can be found in Thessalonians and in Ephesians) and was the label which Quakers called themselves, before they were known as 'Friends of Truth' or 'the people of God called in scorn Quakers'; the term 'Religious Society of Friends' emerged more than a century later. 'While ye have Light, believe in the Light, that ye may be the children of Light,' says Jesus in John's gospel. George Fox refers to this passage in his Journal (p. 16) describing John as the greatest human prophet – John's gospel is often called the Quaker gospel – and saying how John did 'bear witness to the light, which Christ the great heavenly prophet hath enlightened every man [and presumably woman] that cometh into the world withal, that they might believe in it, and become children of light'. This idea, which comes early in Fox's ministry, was however, not original to him. Fox encountered several groups who called themselves 'children of the light' in Nottinghamshire when he visited the area at the start of his ministry. These were former Baptists who were led by Elizabeth Hooton who became Fox's spiritual mentor in this period. By the early 1650s indeed, there were numerous groups across the north of England calling themselves 'children of the light' and they were to become the nuclei of the movement that burst out of the North-West in June 1652 and that came to be known as Quaker. 'In their resolute obedience to all the demands which the Light made upon them and in their sure insight into Truth the early Friends… abundantly justified their name of children of the light,' writes

William Braithwaite, historian of early Quakerism.

The Light Within

What did these first Quakers mean when they called
themselves 'children of light'? The idea of Light is of course at
the heart of all faiths; most faiths, I suspect, would claim to be
'children of light' in one form or another. At the centre of
this is the idea of light as revelation, representing truth against
the darkness of error, of light as an aid, of it saving us when
we are in danger, showing us right and wrong, guiding us to
safety out of danger, and as something that gives comfort
against fear. It is in this sense light as a candle, something we
draw close to in time of trouble. Yet for Early Friends, as their
name 'children of light' suggests, light was something
absolutely fundamental to their witness. It was what they were
about. 'A people that walked in darkness has seen a great
light' (Isaiah 9.1). The central insight of these Friends, their
distinctive contribution to Christian spirituality, lay in the idea
of light, or as they called it, the Light Within. It became (and I
would suggest still is) Quakerism's distinguishing feature.
From this insight all else in Quakerism flowed.

Let us consider what these first Quakers understood by the
Light Within. These children of light stressed the absolute
paramountcy of the direct experience of the Light Within
over everything – over priestly teaching and over scripture –
as the source of religious authority. In its rejection of the
primacy of scripture Quakerism broke with the Protestantism
of its time. Primacy lay with the direct experience of
encounter with God as expressed in the idea of the Light in
John's gospel, and this took precedence over all other
intermediaries between God and humankind. 'Your teacher is
within you, look not forth,' said George Fox, '…for the Lord
God alone will teach his people.'

But what was this Light Within? One thing it was not was the individual conscience or individual reason. Conscience and reason change and vary between individuals, said these Early Friends. The Light Within does not; it is constant and the same for all. It illuminates conscience but it is not conscience. It was not a human phenomenon at all. It was best expressed in the form 'the Inward Light' i.e. something that shines from outside the individual but *into* him or her. I stress this, for these Friends the Inward Light began *outside* the individual and shone inwards. It was not a human creation, dependent ultimately on human reason, but something that came from outside humanity.

The Light can be seen as the ability all humans have to know that God is speaking to us and to understand what God is saying. It is our capacity to understand God's way. As Edmondson put it, it is 'God's witness in our hearts'. Fox famously described this as 'that of God within' but the point being that it came from God not humankind. As Isaac Penington (one of the most prominent Friends to write on the Light Within) said, 'there is a witness of and from God in every conscience'. William Dewsbury, appealing in 1655 to English soldiers in Ireland to join Quakers, wrote 'God is light and has lightened every one of you… when you act against this light… you crucify the life of Christ'. To put it at its starkest, the Light Within is the capacity we all have to respond to God if only we would listen, and the capacity we *all* (I stress all) have to respond to our fellow men and women's needs: it is our divine desire to do good to others.

For Early Friends the Light Within was indeed like a candle in the dark, but also like a lighthouse, speaking to the world. It was a guide: it 'teaches you' said Fox. In doing this it guides you to God. By guiding you to God it leads you to dwell in the Light, to love the Light, to mind the Light, to obey the Light, to walk in the Light: all these are phrases Fox uses.

Early Friends were clear what this guide – this Inward Light – was. It was Christ. As Fox called him, 'Christ the Light' or 'The True Light'. Edmondson, when ministering in Derry, called it 'the Light of Christ in their hearts'. 'If ye love the Light, ye love Christ,' Fox wrote, 'if ye hate that, ye hate Christ,' going on to add, 'I directed people to their inward teacher, Christ.' He described elsewhere 'the light of Jesus Christ that shines in each and every one of your consciences'. It was Fox's realisation of this – that, as he put it, there was 'one even Christ Jesus' that could speak to his condition – that marked his convincement experience at the start of his ministry. He did not need priests, professors or ministers, nor churchly services or creeds or hymns, nor for that matter scripture. The direct, personal experience of Christ through the Inward Light was all that mattered.

This raises the question of how we can be sure that we receive the Inward Light? We should note here that Early Friends said that the Light was open to all; it was not restricted to a pre-determined elite of saved as opposed to the damned. Unlike Protestant churches, Quakers were not Calvinists. The Inward Light was open to all human beings and all could be saved by it. Even those who had never heard of Christ, said Early Friends, could live lives in accordance with the Light Within. John 1.9 makes this clear too: the Light is for all. 'For I saw that Christ died for all men,' wrote Fox, and this is echoed in Penington's comment above, about God being in every conscience. The Inward Light is open to us all. And how do we receive it? Penington answers this by saying it was up to God: we just do. Through faith. 'Why thus,' he writes, 'the Lord opened my spirit.' But it is then up to us to respond to it. 'It is an inward change,' says Penington, 'by the spirit and power of the living God.'

Penington's reference to this 'inward change' is an important aspect of the Light. It brings out the revelation aspect of the

Light, its capacity to reveal things as they are. This is light as more than a candle or even a lighthouse. As Rex Ambler, a contemporary Quaker, has written, the Light is a searchlight turned inward on us, that reveals things we would rather leave hidden, that asks searching questions of us, a light from which there is no escape, no matter how much denial we hide behind. This 'struggle of self-judgement', as Ambler calls it, is a difficult experience that we would do anything to avoid, but which it is ultimately impossible to escape. 'Let the light of Jesus Christ that shines in every one of your consciences, search you thoroughly,' said Fox; echoing this, Edmondson asked for the Lord 'to search me thoroughly'. This is a desperately uncomfortable and difficult experience of self-honesty, but one that Early Friends said you had to go through as part of your convincement. It reflects their emphasis on human broken-ness and the necessity of our first acknowledging our broken-ness if we are to be healed and to grow. 'For the great day of the Lord has come… when every heart will be disclosed and the secrets of everyone's heart will be revealed by the light of Jesus,' said Fox. The consequence of our acceptance of the Light can thus best be summed up in the idea that it changes our lives. It leads, as Penington says, to inward change in us as individuals. Living in the Light was transforming and ultimately life changing.

This encounter with the Light is about something deep within us and about our relationship with God. It says profound things about us as human beings, and about God; it says weighty things about how we see ourselves and about how we see our relationship with God. It says powerful things about our very intimate core, about the depths of our beings, about our very innermost sense of ourselves. It is my view that we all in this room, Quaker and non-Quaker alike, have, at one time or another – and some of us more often than others – been aware of the presence of God in our lives in the way these children of light were when they experienced Christ as the Light Within. It is an experience we find difficult to put into words, but it is the sudden awareness of encounter, the flash of revelation, the sense of not being alone but of being 'accompanied' in our lives that we all so often have.

The Light as encountered by the children of light is therefore a spiritual transformation within the individual. But for Early Friends the Light also had important spiritual implications for life in the world more broadly. There are three aspects to this and I would like now to examine these in turn.

The Light and the World

i) *The Lamb's War of good against evil.* Central to Early Friends' beliefs was the idea of struggle and conflict. This was on both a global and an individual level. The world was consumed by a cosmic struggle of good and evil, they said. So too was the individual. There was a struggle of good and evil within, just as there was without; Edmondson writes of how he 'travailed under a great war and conflict'. This struggle Early Friends called 'the Lamb's War' after the war in the Book of Revelation (chaps 14-19). This was not an outward war of weapons but an inward war, an inner Armageddon, in human hearts, a war of the spirit, a war between the spirit and the 'fleshly world', between Christ and Satan. This war, said Friends, occurs inside us all, when we accept the Light Within as guiding our lives. It is a constant war, one that never ends. It is a war that involves recognising the sharp distinction between good and evil, between Truth and error, between the spirit and the world; there can be no compromise between the two sides.

This Lamb's War begins with our surrender to the Light

Within. 'Give over thine own willing,' said Penington, 'give over thine own running, give over thine own desiring to know or to be anything and sink down into the seed which God sows in the heart and let that grow in thee and breathe in thee and act in thee and thou shalt find by sweet experience that the Lord knows that and loves and owns that and will lead it to the inheritance of life which is his portion.'

We have simply, to make a choice, a commitment. We have to decide whose side we are on, that of the Light or that of the profane world. Are we to live in the Spirit or in the world? Early Friends made that choice: a choice to reject the profane world 'which wars against the Spirit of God', said Fox. Instead they chose to live their lives in the Spirit, as they termed it, within the world yet outside it. They were a people called to be different, to be dangerous, a people called to live outside the world and to recognise that, as Nayler put it, 'if you are at peace in the world's ways… you are not in God's kingdom'. This had two consequences. Firstly, it led them to that plainness that so characterised Early Friends: the acceptance of Quaker grey, of Quaker dress and the rejection of the world's fashions, speech, honours etc, and everything else that went with them, even to their refusal to say 'Good morning' to non-Quakers or to eat at the same table with them. All these were signs of their rejection of the world and their decision to live in the Spirit while in the world, abiding by God's laws only. 'The fleshly mind, spirit and will… lives in disobedience and doth not keep within the law of the Spirit,' said Fox. All other things were irrelevant in comparison. Secondly it led to Early Friends' stress on their perfectibility, something others at the time found difficult to accept. Their view was that once they rejected the world and lived in the Spirit, they were entering into the same Spirit as the Apostles had lived in. This did not mean they did not sin, but did mean they had become, as they put it, 'as Saints'.

The existence of Light implies the existence of darkness. The struggle between the two – Light and Dark – is the Lamb's War. Ultimately, we know, the Light will win. This leads into my second point, the children of light's idea of the Kingdom of Heaven on earth.

ii) The Kingdom of God here on earth. For early Quakers their encounter with the Light made them realise that the Kingdom of God was something that was to be experienced here on earth and not in heaven. 'They said that he (God) was above the skies, calling it heaven,' said William Dewsbury in 1655, 'but I felt the hand of the Lord *within* me' (my emphasis). The Light created, said Fox, a new Creation here on earth, a new Creation that begins in individuals. Francis Howgill again: 'All was overturned… and then I saw the cross of Christ and stood in it… *and the new man was made* and so peace came to be made' (my emphasis). This is a change in the individual, generated by the Light. Howgill is saying here that humans, once they accept the Light, can transcend their humanity, and that this is not something that has to wait for a resurrection in the future or in heaven or in the sky. He continues: 'and the Lord appeared daily to us, to our Astonishment, Amazement and Great Admiration, in so much that we often said one to another with great joy of heart "what, is the Kingdom of God come to be with men?"'

These Quakers identified this Kingdom of God as existing here in a corporal reality on earth and they found it in two experiences. One was in their experience of God as expressed in the Light Within and the personal communion of deep intimacy between the individual and God, that they realised could be experienced by anyone at anytime and in any place. This was living in the Spirit. 'For behold the Kingdom of God is within you,' it says in Luke (17.21). This Kingdom of God existed within each and every one of us, said Early Quakers, and could be identified in our individual capacity to find Christ and experience his living reality in our lives. The second experience lay in community. For Early Quakers the Kingdom of God was to be experienced in the solidarity of the Christian community, among Friends, both in Meeting for Worship where the Light was experienced at its most intense, and outside it. As Howgill's statement about the Lord appearing among men reveals, a solidarity emerged in the ties of Christian sentiment between like-minded people seeking God together, so that Christ's presence became real and the Kingdom of God thus existed in tangible, incarnate form ('What? Come to be with men?'). In this dual experience of the Light, God's presence becomes a reality and we experience a living Pentecost, not once in Palestine but repeatedly, everyday and everywhere. The encounter with God was beyond space. When we decide to live in the Spirit we experience a transcendent God that exists in the world and that can be found wherever we choose to look.

This, it must be admitted, does not come easy. It requires an acceptance of our broken-ness and our human limitations if we are to know God. In short, it requires us to accept our humanity but in doing so, this bring us the presence of God. To live in the spirit therefore, to take sides in the Lamb's War with the implications of personal change it generates, is to go beyond our human nature to something beyond humanity, to an encounter with God that transforms us all. For the reconciliation that the children of light achieved, I believe, was not simply between humanity and God but also within humanity, between individuals and just as importantly, within ourselves. This reconciliation was not something that occurred 'above the skies' or in a future resurrection but here and now. It is an inner apocalypse indeed, an inner transformation that Early Quakers strived for, one that changes us as people.

The idea of the Kingdom of God being here on earth, in the life in the Spirit – that the Kingdom of God is beyond *space* –

leads us to the third aspect of the Light I want to examine, that which concerns *time*.

iii) The presence of God now. Throughout the writings of Early Quakers is their awareness of the presence of God, as mediated through Jesus, in their lives and in the world around them. Having experienced God through the Inward Light, the awareness of God was a real, tangible and immediate encounter for these people. Edmondson wrote how in Dublin, 'the Lord's presence appeared mightily among us'. Richard Wailer, while in prison in Waterford in 1656, wrote that 'the Lord is risen among us in his mighty power'. God's presence was not something these children of light read about in books or listened to in ministry but something they physically experienced. God's presence had the impact of a physical shock on them. It was their desire to tremble at the overwhelming presence of the Lord that led to their scornful nickname, the 'Quakers'; rarely has a description been more appropriate.

This physical and personal earthquake at the presence of God reflected their surrender to the demands of the Light and that they had experienced the Quaker Pentecost. Thomas Kelly, an American Quaker, 300 years later wrote that these Early Friends were 'burning for God', giving up their own wills to do God's will as expressed in the teachings of Christ. This was a physically frightening experience yet also a comforting one: as in Francis Howgill's sublime testimony that he was 'lost in the incomprehensible being of eternal love'. Becoming aware of the immediate presence of God implied an awareness of God's love for us as individuals, no matter who we are or what we might have done. God's love was both incomprehensible and eternal, but was there for us all. He was a God who was *there*. Or rather, a God who was *here*. This is the central mystery of the Christian faith and was the central message of these children of light.

Early Quakers explained this mystery in terms of the Second Coming of Christ. The central teaching of the children of light is summed up in Fox's statement 'for Christ is come to teach his people himself'. There is no more fundamental statement of Quaker belief than this, and it was at the heart of what the children of light understood as Light. Their experience of the Light made them realise that 'Christ is come and is coming' as they said; he was here, now. We could all have a direct personal relationship with Christ. This Second Coming was not something that would happen in the future, but was something that was happening now, immediately, that happened and happens as soon as we open ourselves to the presence of God. Fox's idea was of a 'new Creation' that would close the gap between God and the broken-ness of humanity that derives from our human inadequacy. This new Creation occurs within us when we realise that 'Christ is come to teach his people himself'. This new Creation ends the alienation of humankind from the presence of God, that alienation from God that derived from the very fact of our *human* nature. This experience of a new Creation – of a new humanity, of the kingdom of heaven on earth – is something we can all experience and experience now, in the immediate present and not the future. It is a new Creation that occurs within our hearts when we resolve to slough off the old self with its egotism and selfishness and open ourselves to Christ. This new Creation is the transformation of our selves that occurs at that moment we accept the presence of Christ in our lives. It is an inner apocalypse, or what Douglas Gwyn, the Quaker writer, calls 'the Quaker apocalypse'.

'For Christ is come to teach his people himself,' with its *present* tense, is thus the key Quaker teaching, the Quaker contribution to Christian theology. The realisation of the meaning of those words – that the Second Coming of Christ to create the kingdom of heaven occurs now in the present and the here – was the pivotal moment in the emergence of Quakerism. It is also the pivotal moment in all our lives. It is that moment when the Light makes us aware that we live, all of us, accompanied lives and that we are not alone on this earth. It is the moment we realise that God *is*, and that life has a purpose, even if that purpose seems at times difficult and bewildering. Like Howgill we can then exclaim, 'what, is the Kingdom of God come to be with men?' 'It is, Friend,' we reply, 'for Christ is come to teach his people himself.'

The immediate presence – of God here and now – is thus the third element of the insights of the children of light that I wish to emphasise in my attempt to define Quakerism. In essence it is the idea that the encounter with God is timeless and beyond time, it is in deep time, in the deep present. For these children of light, in their new relationship with God, *time* and its manifestations (past, present and future), just like space, were fused as one in the *now*.

The Experience of Encounter

You may feel that this attempt to define the beliefs of Early Friends is of historical interest but no more, that it has only limited relevance for today's Society of Friends. I would suggest that it does in fact have a lot to say to us today. What is this? What do these children of light have to say to us – Quaker and non-Quaker alike – today?

What unites all of these aspects of the Light is that at the heart of the Quaker spiritual experience is an overwhelming sense of encounter with God. Their writings drip with the presence of God. God is not some distant figure, intellectualised in theological precepts or in a Sunday sermon, or written in words on a page, but a living reality in their lives. God is a living presence in their lives, here in the ever present. For these Early Quakers, God is. God is immediate. Here. Immanent. Inescapable.

> 'Whither shall I go from thy spirit? Or whither shall I flee from thy presence? If I ascend up into heaven, thou art there: if I make my bed in hell, behold, thou art there. If I take the wings of the morning, and dwell in the uttermost parts of the sea: even there shall thy hand lead me, and thy right hand shall hold me.' (Psalm 139).

Further, the encounter they experienced is a profoundly intimate one, of a God who is here with us, and this intimacy is something I want to stress. This God can be experienced in every second of our lives, wherever we are, 'for Christ is come'. This God is infinite yet also intimate, close and personal. A God who accompanies us, understands us and stands by us. As in any intimate relationship, this intimate encounter with God that Early Friends proclaimed, changes the individual.

It does this in two ways. The first way is best described in the word surrender. Early Friends spoke of how their experience of convincement was accompanied by surrender to the Other – to God's will. This indeed is what we Quakers still do in the silence of Meeting for Worship. When entering into the silence we too surrender to God's Will We wait on God's Will, not our own, accepting that we will go where the Meeting will take us. 'Therefore wait patiently upon the Lord whatsoever condition you may be in,' said Fox, 'wait in the Grace and Truth that comes by Jesus, for if you do so, there is a promise to you and the Lord God will fulfil it in you... Wait upon God in that which is pure, though you see little and know little and have little and see your emptiness... stand still in it everyone to see your Saviour.'

Central to this waiting that Fox talks of is our need to

surrender our ego: the intimacy of our relationship with God is one that takes us out of our selves, suppresses our ego and leads us to surrender to God's Will. This indeed, is the theme of all the great religions: whether Islam, Judaism, Buddhism or whatever. As quoted above, 'give over thine own willing… give over thine own desiring,' said Penington. It is what Thomas Kelly calls 'Holy Obedience'. If we do so follow our encounter with God with this Holy Obedience – this surrender of ourselves to God's Will – then we enter into a special place within ourselves: deep, private, intimate, quiet, safe. We are, as Francis Howgill said above, 'lost in the incomprehensible being of eternal love'.

If surrender is the first consequence of our encounter with God then confidence is the second. We are strengthened by our encounter with the Other because we now know what matters. This confidence is best captured by Fox's description of the Two Oceans, 'I saw the infinite love of God. I saw also that there was an ocean of darkness and death, but an infinite ocean of light and love, which flowed over the ocean of darkness. And in that also I saw the infinite love of God.' It is the knowledge of which ocean will win out in the end – though it may take time and many stormy waves – that leads us into the joy that lies at the heart of the Quaker faith, best seen in Fox's statement that his encounter with Christ meant that his heart 'did leap with joy'.

At the centre of this experience of light that the children of light lived through was therefore the idea of an encounter with God – a God who is there – and how that experience of intimate encounter changed them and changed how they lived in the world. On this, if nothing else, all traditions within Quakerism can unite. Here, I suggest, is that essence of Quakerism I set out to define at the start of this lecture. It was an encounter that led to an experience of atonement, redemption and personal convincement. It drove them to great things. It led William Edmondson to jail in Armagh, Derry, Cavan and elsewhere and to the public stocks in Belturbet. It led our fore-fathers and fore-mothers, the Irish children of light, to their work in the Famine, to their enterprise in industry and philanthropy, and to their pioneering work in education. It led to the witness that the Margery Atkinsons of our Society have expressed over the centuries. It poses questions for us today.

Conclusion

I want finally to return to where I started this lecture, with reflections on our 350th anniversary. I speak now to the Quakers in this room. What are the implications of this examination of the children of light for today's Society of Friends? We have, after all, moved on and changed, and in many ways rightly so. The Society of Friends today is very different to what it was in William Edmondson and Margery Atkinson's time. Yet I think these children of light have much still to say to us today. In their rejection of priestly hierarchies and scriptural fundamentalism, of the labels of church identities whether Catholic or Protestant, they point us to the essence of Christ's message, that life on earth is about encounter, what they described as the encounter with light, the light of God. 'Art thou a child of light?' asked Fox, 'and hast thou walked in the light?' This question remains as true today as in 1654. In their description of the Light Within they spelt out for us the message of that intimate relationship between humankind and God, between self and other, that lies within everyone of us in this room tonight.

I believe that the experience of these children of light tells us that we have a need to readdress our spirituality. This is not at the expense of service to our fellow human beings, but alongside it. As Christians, we ignore our spirituality at our peril. Service, or good works, without the spiritual bedrock of the light become like the house built on sand without foundations, destroyed when the storm comes. The encounter of Early Friends with the Light shows us that life in this world is about an encounter with God, an encounter in the here and now, in the present time and in the present place. It shows us that the Second Coming has arrived, that it occurs every minute of every day. God is immanent in the world, not just 2,000 years ago in Galilee but today in Waterford as much as anywhere else. For we all *can* lead accompanied lives and lives of Light, whatever our faith might be and whatever the tradition within which we choose to express it.

I speak as a Quaker and as someone who is grateful 'beyond what words can utter' that I found Quakerism and Quakerism found me. This study of the children of light, I hope, tells us that we have a precious heritage that we would be foolish to ignore. This year we celebrate the 350th anniversary of the arrival of Quakerism on this island. We must, I accept, go forward as a Society and not spend our time looking backwards. But 350 years is an appropriate time to reflect on where our corporate faith is heading. Those Early Quakers still speak to us down the centuries. Are we listening? As Alastair Heron, a contemporary Quaker and one of the most perceptive commentators on British Quakerism, has recently written, 'I have no doubt that the Religious Society of Friends in Britain is facing serious difficulties. These are not primarily structural or organisational but spiritual.' I suspect he is right and that these problems in Britain are reflected, to a greater or lesser extent, throughout Quakerism in the North Atlantic world. We are members of a Society of Friends that has become, in my view, essentially secularised, that has become, as Thomas Kelly put it more than half a century ago, 'mildly and conventionally religious'. We are now, in the words of Harvey Gillman (a contemporary Quaker), 'a well-intentioned social club of like-minded, nice people'. That is not meant as a compliment. Thomas Kelly again, 'We are secular and secularism is in our Meeting Houses.' Christine Trevett in her Swarthmore lecture of 1997 is right, that if George Fox was to reappear among us and ask his celebrated question, 'what canst thou say?' our answer all too often would be 'er, um, well, not very much, George, not very much'.

We Quakers in Ireland have a precious heritage of an encounter with God some 350 years ago, of the way that encounter changed the lives of William Edmondson and Margery Atkinson. Their experience still speaks to us. We need to have more confidence in proclaiming that encounter, in accepting it as central to our lives and our faith. For I am convinced that Christ is still come to teach his people himself. The light proclaimed by those children of light in 1654 still shines on us today. Those children of light, like children everywhere, have much to teach us: they question, they challenge, they cause us pain and difficulty as we adjust to their challenges, but they, again like children everywhere, also show trust and faith and love and joy and confidence in the future. Let us, on this 350th anniversary, become like children: children of light.

Sources used

R. Ambler, *Truth of the Heart (London, 2001)*

E. Brimelow, *In and Out the Silence* (London, 1989)

B.P. Dandelion, D. Gwyn and T. Peat, *Heaven on Earth* (Birmingham, 1998)

The Journal of George Fox, ed. J.L. Nickalls, (London, 1952)

H. Gillman and A. Heron (eds), *Searching the Depths* (London, 1996)

G. Gorman, *The Amazing Fact of Quaker Worship* (London, 1993)

D. Gwyn, *Apocalypse of the Word* (Richmond, IN, 1986)

D. Gwyn, *Seekers Found* (Wallingford, PA, 2000)

T. Kelly, *The Eternal Promise* (New York, 1966)

T. Kelly, *A Testament of Devotion* (London, 1979)

J. Lampen (ed), *Wait in the Light, the Spirituality of George Fox* (London, 1981)

R. Moore, *The Light in their Consciences* (Pennsylvania, 2000)

I. Penington, *The Light Within* (Philadelphia, nd)

Quaker Faith and Practice (London, 1995)

D.V. Steere (ed), *Quaker Spirituality* (London, 1984)

C. Trevett, *Previous Convictions* (London, 1997)